PR⸍   ⸜OURCE

"An excellent resource for the newly single parent—one that is there
for you when you need it."

Practical

"Finally,   ⸍hich not
only prov   ut recog-
nizes the   ⸍k you,
thank yo⸍

⸍g Alliance

"A wonc   ⸍very single
parent ai   sy to read,
well orga   ⸍arenting.
Helpful ⸍   ⸍e this lifestyle a lit

⸍on

"Address⸍   ⸍orth buying
the book   ⸍riceless tips
on elimi⸍   ⸍ent burnout.
A must f⸍

Mary Kalifon, Director
Parent-Child Resources
Cedars-Sinai Health Systems, Los Angeles

⸍*ork There*

"No single parent should be without this valuable resource."
> Andrea Engber, co-author of *The Complete Single Mother,* Director & Founder of the National Organization for Single Mothers, Inc. and Contributing Editor, *Working Mother* magazine

"[The] handbook covers the most important concerns of single parents throughout the country, economically presenting the issues and lavishing tips, techniques and strategies for gaining mastery over them. Although the perspective they emphasize is that of the single parent, any parent might benefit from adopting the practical solutions they advance. In addition to its relevant and substantive content, the guide is especially noteworthy because it is so readable: deftly written, upbeat but never patronizing, concise and detailed..."
> *Booklist*

"While time, money and energy are three elements in short supply in most households, *The Single Parent Resource* is a guide to organizing a menage when all are at a premium."
> *Publishers Weekly*

"I wish a book such as *The Single Parent Resource* has been available to me when I was a single mother of two young children 15 years ago! Brook Noel and Art Klein have done the world of single parenthood a great service by creating such a thorough, compassionate resource. I am putting the book on the top of the resource list I hand out to all parents going through divorce. As a psychotherapist I found the chapter on *Transforming Difficult Emotions* to be extremely well done, and the information in *Improving Your Children's Emotional Health* to be particularly outstanding. *The Single Parent Resource* should help save the sanity of many a stressed single parent and smooth the development of the children they love!"

"A well-organized and clear book written with an eye to the practical. Any single parent would be grateful to have this book on her bookshelf and will refer to it again and again."

"An important resource for every single parent...valuable information at your fingertips all the time. I will add a copy to my list of references for all single parents."

"*The Single Parent Resource* is a wonderful tool that offers guidance and insight into the challenges that single parents face."

"*The Single Parent Resource* is an invaluable guide for those either newly single or on their own for a while. The step-by-step approach and countless tips make this guide quick to read and easy to implement."

"I wish that every single parent in San Angelo, Texas could receive a copy of *The Single Parent Resource* and leave it by their bed, desk, chair, etc., to use daily. I am not a single parent, but there were so many practical items for ANY parent.

Through my reading I feel that it impacted me not only as a publisher of a local family magazine, but as a parent. Beginning today I will be more in control of my life in a very positive way because of the benefits of this book."

Carolyn Harper
Owner/Publisher
San Angelo Family Magazine

"*The Single Parent Resource* is a rich collection of practical and hopeful advice, solutions to everyday problems, and best of all, support for the single parent who wants to get their life back on track without short-changing the kids..."

Judith Shervan, Ph.D. & James Sniechowski, Ph.D. authors of *The New Intimacy: Discovering the Magic at the Heart of Your Differences*

THE SINGLE PARENT RESOURCE

THE SINGLE PARENT RESOURCE

BROOK NOEL
WITH ART KLEIN

CHAMPION PRESS, LTD.
BEVERLY HILLS

CHAMPION PRESS, LTD.
BEVERLY HILLS, CALIFORNIA

Library of Congress Catalog Card Number 97-76841

Cataloging-in-Publication Data
Noel, Brook.
      The single parent resource / by Brook Noel with Art Klein. —1st ed.
      p. cm.
      Includes index.
      Preassigned LCCN: 97-76841
      ISBN: 1-891400-44-4

      1. Parenting 2. Single parents. I. Klein, Arthur C.
  II. Title.
      HQ759.915.N64 1998
      QB197-41480

Manufactured in the United States of America
10 9 8 7 6 5 4 3 2

Cover photograph by Harriet Stowers.
Back cover photograph by Mary S. Toth of Portraits Today, Port Washington, Wisconsin.
Book Design by Pilot Publishing, Milwaukee, Wisconsin.

TO ALL THE SINGLE PARENTS
WHO INVESTED IN THIS BOOK,
WHO IN TURN INVESTED IN THEMSELVES,
AND IN TURN INVESTED IN THEIR CHILDREN-

THE FUTURE'S CHILDREN.

ABOUT THIS BOOK

Although this book is written by two people, it is told from Brook Noel's point of view.

PRONOUN USAGE

The pronouns "he" and "she" are used alternately throughout this book to avoid the wordiness or using "his or her" or the more formal approach of always using the masculine pronoun.

A NOTE TO OUR BUSY SINGLE PARENT READERS

Each chapter in this book is complete in and of itself. We encourage single parents, who are too busy to read this book cover to cover, to start at the chapter overviews in Chapter One and move immediately to whatever chapter concerns them most. Nothing will be lost by reading the chapters out of order or over a period of time.

A NOTE ABOUT RESOURCES

The authors do not specifically endorse or promote any reference listed within this book, unless specifically stated.

QUOTATIONS

Most single parent quotes, within this book, are printed and attributed as specified by the single parent who provided the quote. In instances where single parents could not be reached, the authors credited the quote to "single mother" or "single father."

ABOUT THE AUTHORS

Brook Noel is an author, publisher and speaker about topics pertaining to single parenting. From the age of eight-months-old, Brook was raised in a single-parent home by her mother. Currently, she resides in Vancouver, Washington.

Art Klein is an East Hampton-based author. For several years he was the single father of two children. He has authored five books, three of which were Book of the Month Club selections. Art speaks in myriad public forums about the value of two parents in children's lives.

Although this book was written by two people, it is told from Brook Noel's point of view.

The authors welcome your comments, questions and suggestions for future editions.

Please write to:
Brook Noel
c/o Champion Press, Ltd.
264 S. La Cienega Blvd., Suite 1064
Beverly Hills, CA 90211

ACKNOWLEDGMENTS

This book has been in the making for seven years. Throughout these years I have spoken with many single parents and their children. While I could never list you all by name, I'd like to thank each and every one of you and wish your family continued success and growth.

I would like to acknowledge the following friends and professionals who offered their thoughtful assistance with this manuscript in one or more of its stages: Pat Feinman and Nan Grossbarth for their meticulous and thoughtful editing. Mary Ann Klotz, whose friendship has truly been a blessing, and whose dedication and belief in me has helped me to reach places that I could never reach alone. Andy, who understood how much this all meant to me and stood behind me during the long process. A crew of people I met in Maui in 1996, who helped me in ways I'd never have imagined. Scott and Jill, for always telling me this was a good idea and encouraging me and my work. Art, who never stopped reminding me that I could do anything I set my mind and heart to. My brother, Caleb, for his help in the early stages of both my life and my newsletter publishing for single parents. And, my mother, I give you a standing ovation.

Thank you all.

Brook Noel

CONTENTS

CHAPTER ONE
MOVING AHEAD:
HELP FOR SINGLE PARENTS STARTS HERE...25

CHAPTER TWO
NAVIGATING THE SINGLE-PARENT LIFE...31

CHAPTER THREE
MANAGING THE SINGLE-PARENT HOUSEHOLD...61

CHAPTER FOUR
BALANCING WORK AND FAMILY...79

CHAPTER FIVE: PART ONE
CREATING A SOLID FINANCIAL PLAN...91

CHAPTER FIVE (PART TWO)
CREATING A SOLID FINANCIAL PLAN FOR THE
FUTURE...109

CHAPTER EIGHT
THE SOCIAL LIFE OF THE SINGLE PARENT...159

CHAPTER NINE
COMMITTING TO MAKING
YOUR CUSTODIAL ARRANGEMENT WORK...171

CHAPTER TEN
FINDING QUALITY CHILD CARE...193

CHAPTER ELEVEN
IMPROVING CHILDREN'S EMOTIONAL HEALTH...207

CHAPTER TWELVE
MYTHS AND MUDSLINGING...237

END NOTES

INTRODUCTION

According to the US Bureau of the Census, nearly one out of three families with children are headed by a single parent. Another Bureau of the Census report estimates that 61% of all children will spend all or part of their formative years in households headed by a single parent.

You are, typically, a wage-earning, child-raising, role-modeling miracle worker. But, you are also an individual who, according to our nationwide survey, often cannot get expert answers to your most pressing challenges as a single parent. In fact, a remarkable 98 percent of survey participants said they would like a book that gave them real-life solutions for their day-to-day lives.

We set out to write that book.

Our interest is more than academic. Brook Noel is the publisher of *The Single Parent Resource* and has been writing about single-parenting since the age of sixteen. She has also been raised by a single mom. Art Klein was a single dad for several years and is the author of three Book of the Month Club selections.

Our knowledge is just a starting point though. That's why we conducted a nationwide survey of single parents. We longed to go beyond the "crisis period" of transforming to a single-parent household. We wanted to seek out the answers for facing the day-to-day challenges of this household. It was critically important for us to find out what type of help you felt you needed. After extensive interviews through phone, e-mail and in-person—this book contains a kind of wisdom you won't find anywhere else—the collective advice and thoughts of single parents themselves.

There was one more dimension we wanted to add to this book. For certain topics that are both complex and essential—from dealing with stress to balancing a budget—we felt you should have access to the advice of experts in those areas. We've included these resources.

The outcome is a book we hope will help you with every key aspect of your life. A guide you can refer to time and time again. A friend in need. And a resource that is there for you with answers when you need them.

You're always helping others—your kids and your neighbors' kids, your friends and relatives, schools and organizations. We hope this book gives you something back.

Welcome to our book.

And thank you for joining us on this incredible and future-shaping journey of single parenting.

SUMMARY OF THE TOP TEN CONCERNS OF SINGLE PARENTS

*The top ten concerns of single parents, as reported
in a nationwide survey of 500 single parents, are:*

- How can I better navigate the day-to-day challenges of life as a single parent?
- How can I manage my single-parent household more effectively?
- How can I successfully balance work and family?
- How can I prepare a solid financial plan and budget system for both the present and the future?
- How can I handle the difficult day-to-day emotions I feel?
- How can I create a helpful support network for myself and my family?
- How can I improve my social life and interaction as a single parent?
- How can I maximize my current custodial arrangement?
- How can I find the best quality child care?
- How can I better understand and improve my child's emotional health?

The answers to these questions can be found in the pages ahead...

CHAPTER ONE
MOVING AHEAD

Getting to where you are now—a single parent raising one or more children—is an extraordinary achievement. It takes phenomenal will and skill, understanding and love, to make the transition to single parenthood. Even more to your credit, chances are that you already have accomplished what two-parent families working together often find difficult enough: establishing a stable home and a well-nurtured environment of safety for children.

Not that it's been all roses for you, of course. Single parenting is many things—from demanding and downright exhausting to joyous and immensely satisfying. But it's by no means easy.

Still, you've made it through a divorce. Or chosen to go it alone as a single parent. Or weathered the loss of a mate. Which means that you already have substantial inner strengths and life skills.

Now the question is: What practical steps can you take—right away—to substantially improve your own life as a single parent and enrich the lives of your children?

We asked that very same question of single parents. Indeed, we asked single parents a wide range of questions by questionnaire and by telephone. (One thing we found out for sure: single parents are the most patient individuals on the planet for taking the time to answer questions! It must be because they get so much practice in dealing with their children's questions alone!)

The input we got from our single parent survey participants represents an incredibly rich and relevant mine of practical solutions and insights that mirrors your life and addresses your most timely concerns.

Relevant is the key word. The content in the chapters ahead has the potential to improve the quality of your life from awakening to bedtime. Instead of trying to cover every topic related to single-parenting, we sought the top concerns of single parents. Then we addressed each one in depth and backed it with expert sources and resources. Each chapter that follows will thoroughly explore one of the top ten challenges and contain or conclude with a resource section.

Most important of all, the answers you'll find are primarily from individuals who have "walked the walk"–single parents who have been there themselves and who, collectively, have acquired through their firing-line experience a kind of wisdom that no one else can have. This wealth of wisdom is accentuated by the collective input of experts from a wide variety of fields. From accountants to counselors, from authors to teachers, we left no stone unturned in our quest for the answers today's single parents seek.

Before diving into the life-changing strategies contained herein, we suggest you take a moment and look at the highlights of the upcoming chapters. As you read through the knowledge revealed in each chapter, place a checkmark next to any that are particularly relevant to your current single-parent experience. Each chapter is complete in itself, so if you need immediate help use this section as a springboard to guide you to advice. Or read the book straight through, then go back and give extra attention to the chapters you have identified as key interests.

Grab a pencil and get ready to start changing your life for the better. Check all the areas and concerns which affect your life the most.

☐ NAVIGATING THE SINGLE-PARENT LIFE
(See Chapter Two)
Solutions include: How to build a foundation that gives you

greater energy and purpose on a daily basis; the importance of a balance wheel and priority system; how to fit more rest and exercise into the most pressure-packed schedule; creating a discovery system to recharge your passion for life.

❒ **MANAGING THE SINGLE-PARENT HOUSEHOLD**
(See Chapter Three)
Solutions include: How every single parent can immediately be a better household manager; how to simplify the life of your household; create a Communication Central station to maximize family effectiveness; how to cook once a month and still have thirty home-cooked meals; avoiding common household pitfalls.

❒ **BALANCING WORK AND FAMILY**
(See Chapter Four)
Solutions include: The single greatest key to successfully balancing work and family; a "pooling" strategy for giving you more time every day; an innovative way to inspire your children to want to do more work around the home; tips for making your job more compatible with your children's needs; how to look at other careers even when you don't have a free minute; creating a back-up plan for when work interferes with home life; the value of a family happy hour.

❒ **CREATING A SOLID FINANCIAL PLAN AND BUDGET SYSTEM**
(See Chapter Five)
Solutions include: Strategies that almost instantly improve your budget and calm your nerves; simple ways to increase your wealth; the best strategies for long-term savings; how to deal more effectively with complex matters—from health insurance to life insurance to college savings to retirement.

❒ **TRANSFORMING DIFFICULT SINGLE-PARENT EMOTIONS INTO OPPORTUNITIES FOR GROWTH**
(See Chapter Six)

Solutions include: How to tackle the key emotional problems of single parenthood; turning common emotional problems into uncommon opportunities for emotional growth; proven ways to ease fatigue and constructively work out anger and stress from "juggling" work and family; how to handle resentment and self-pity caused by isolation and loneliness; the cleansing process of letting go.

❑ **CREATING A SUPPORT NETWORK**
(See Chapter Seven)
Solutions include: The single greatest key to meeting your need for support; how to find support for your children; single parent network organizations available to you; how to create a single-parent "share" program to save time and money; the rewards of starting your own support network; new ideas for adding dimension to current support groups.

❑ **THE SOCIAL LIFE OF THE SINGLE PARENT**
(See Chapter Eight)
Solutions include: The best ways to break free of isolation patterns; how to give yourself more and have more to give your children; how to sort out conflicting feelings about social times; simple ways to dramatically improve your social life; how to talk to your kids about your social needs; handling romantic interests and overnight guests.

❑ **COMMITTING TO MAKING YOUR CUSTODIAL ARRANGEMENT WORK**
(See Chapter Nine)
Solutions include: The importance of working together; how to move ahead when the other parent won't cooperate; creating productive meetings and agendas; creating common household rules; notes for non-custodial parents; tips on joint custody; single parents' wisdom on making custody work; pitfalls parents need to avoid; explaining another parent's absence.

❏ FINDING QUALITY CHILD CARE

(See Chapter Ten)

Solutions include: A planning method for choosing child care; how to interview child care providers; getting the most out of your child care program; choosing the program that's right for your child; what to watch for as your child begins her new program; help in the search.

❏ IMPROVING CHILDREN'S EMOTIONAL HEALTH

(See Chapter Eleven)

Solutions include: Comforting guidelines for children of different ages; the best ways to improve self-esteem; dealing with the twin blades of depression and anger; handling children's resentment, fear and guilt; healthy outlets for children's anger; keys for effective and rewarding communication.

❏ MYTHS AND MUDSLINGING: SLAMMING THE DOOR ON THE NEGATIVES AND OPENING THE DOOR TO A MORE POSITIVE LIFE

(See Chapter Twelve)

Solutions include: Breaking through society's stereotypes—the facts and reality; the "new" single parent, what the single-parent home means for our future; what we need to do for each other and our children.

Now that you have identified what is most important to you, you're ready to start changing your life for the better! Let's get started.

CHAPTER TWO
NAVIGATING THE
SINGLE-PARENT LIFE

"Just like with airplane oxygen masks—'Put yours
on and then help the child next to you.' You have
to get back on your feet before you can truly be
of help to your child."

Teri Ross
Spring Grove, Pennsylvania

"After meeting the demands of working full time and taking care of
my children, there simply isn't any time left over for myself," said
Julie, the single mother of two teenage sons.

"In theory, creating time for myself is a great idea—in the hustle
and bustle of reality, it's more of a fantasy," said another single
mother.

Lack of time concerns over 90% of our survey participants. Caught
between the demands of work, family and social obligations, single
parents commonly report feeling "out of control," stressed and just
plain overwhelmed. "If I could just balance what is on my plate, my
life would be beautiful," adds Sally, the single mother of three. My
co-author and I set out to find solutions for Sally and other single
parents. *It all begins with you*, was the answer we heard time and time
again. Before a person can organize and structure her own life, she
must first organize and structure herself. Part of this structuring
involves identifying key goals and priorities and aligning your life with
these goals.

As I listened to single parents relay the time struggles that complicated their lives, I was reminded of a conversation I had with a good friend.

While working on two books and establishing a business, my days were always too short, and my stress level was at its peak. I was separated at the time with a two-year-old daughter. The demands on my time were great and the first thing to go, to make room for these demands, was my daily walk. The second thing to go was my attempt at home-cooked meals. I say attempt because I'm the world's worst cook. The third thing I shaved from my day was two hours of sleep. For a month or two this worked well, and then the hectic pace and lack of balance caught up with me. But I felt I had no choice. To meet the demands that were bombarding my life, I had to make more time and that meant less time for myself. Didn't it?

> During the past four years of single parenting, I continually learn and re-learn that taking care of myself first is not selfish, but rather the beginning of harmony in a single-parent (or other) family.
>
> *William Rathbun*
> *Lavina, Montana*

As I relayed this frustration to a friend, he questioned my priorities and the lack of "me time" in my schedule. I informed him that I simply had no choice, I had taken on these commitments and had to make the time for them. Yet he noticed my voice was monotone, and my typical zest for endeavors was fast evaporating. He offered suggestion after suggestion, and I countered each with the same reason: I would feel guilty doing so much for myself when there was so much else that needed tending. Finally, he offered the following anecdote.

"Your house is on fire. You're on the way to an important presentation. You're late, and the deadline is one that could cost you great consequence. But you look back, and there is that house burning. Everything you treasured in your life succumbing to flames. The fire is moving slowly enough that you could get out some of your most prized possessions—of course, this will only make you later for your presentation. What do you do?"

I rolled my eyes. This seemed like an obvious choice. "I'd go back," I replied. "I'm not crazy enough to let all that go over some meeting. " "Would you feel guilty for doubling back?"

"No," I said immediately. "Well, trust me then; your house is on fire. Double back for yourself." I hung up the phone and realized he was right. It was up to me to find the extinguisher to put out the fire and get my life back in balance. It was up to me to make time for life.

THE IMPORTANCE OF BALANCE

Before restructuring your own life, it's important to take stock of where you are currently, and then design a template for where you would like to be. Nancy Buchannon, a psychotherapist at Charter Behavioral Counseling of Milwaukee, offered the following useful and quick method to take stock of your current situation.

Draw a circle.

Consider each of the following six areas:

- Family
- Relationships, friends, social life
- Emotional well-being
- Physical health
- Career
- Spirituality

Number each of these areas by order of importance. Mark the most important with the number one and proceed through six. Then, it's time to design a wheel for how your life is currently balanced. As you look at each of these areas think about your past week. If the week totaled 100 percent, how much time did you devote to each area?

When I created my own balance wheel, based on these directions, I ended up with something like this:

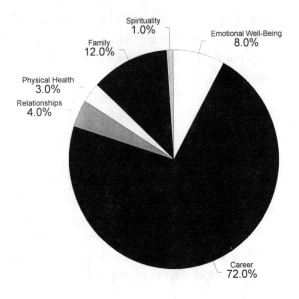

Brook's Sample Balance Wheel

This was an eye opener for me. I had rated my priorities much differently than how I was living. Quickly, I realized why I felt out of balance—I simply was not living life by my own values and priorities.

Take a look at your priority ranking. If you're feeling out of balance, stressed or frustrated, check to see how the wheel matches up with your priorities. Are you devoting too much time to lower priority items and not enough time to the higher ranking items? That factor alone is the single greatest cause of stress and frustration. Fortunately, it's correctable with a little devotion and work.

After identifying where you stand, it's time to imagine how your wheel would look ideally. Make another circle and this time create the perfect wheel for your life. Mine looked something like this:

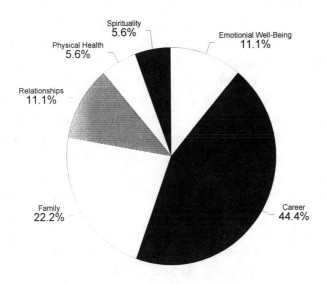

Brook's Ideal Wheel

A few things to remember. Wheels need not be a perfect balance of all six areas. It's common for certain areas to demand more attention or for us to focus on several areas over the others. What matters is creating a wheel that is accurate for a lifestyle that you are comfortable with.

Measure your progress. Because this is such an easy technique, it offers a great way to measure progress. Look at the wheel of where you are and the wheel of how you would like your life to be. In the upcoming weeks try to create a wheel each Sunday night. Watch when you improve and when you fall back. Keep yourself on track.

PRIORITIES AND GOALS:
THE IMPORTANCE OF DIRECTION

In a bit we'll get down to laying out a solid plan for organizing your time and tracking your priorities. First, it's important to completely understand where you are, what obstacles you have been battling, and what strategies you can use to overcome them.

Identifying goals and priorities is vital to a successfully balanced life. Most people have been asked to do this at some point—either in school or at work or as part of a self-improvement program. Still many people get flustered when the topic of goals comes up. Fear of setting goals too high, fear of commitment, and not knowing what course to chart are just a few reasons people shudder at the concept of goals. Yet goals remain an important part of the value system. Imagine leaving Los Angeles with the instructions to go to New York. Obviously, it would be easier to accomplish this with a map. Without a map, the trip would be nearly impossible, or require much more time and effort than the simple process of purchasing a map. Goals work the same way. They allow you to identify where you are and the path to get from one point to the other. The most common pitfall of people designing goals is the failure to use their designs as a map. When goals are recorded and then set aside, this is as useful as putting a map in your glove box, yet expecting to know which road to take. Goals need to be consulted regularly, just like a map, and if you get off course, you need to re-evaluate and make a new plan. To design a goal map, first identify an area of your life where you seek advancement. Use that area to work through the goal process that follows. For this example, I'll use the goal of starting a part-time business for extra income. Here are the steps needed to make the map.

Identify the exact goal. In one sentence, clarify the goal you are aiming to accomplish as specifically as possible. *Example: To open a part-time tax business that brings in $300 a month in extra income (gross).*

Identify a completion date. *My business will be established in eighteen months.*

> Never give up your hopes and dreams. They may take longer to achieve, but in the end the reward is the same.
>
> *Stacy De Carlo*
> *San Jose,*
> *California*

Identify the evolution of the goal. What major points and steps happen during this time period? A. *The basics of establishing a business, permits, licensing, updating certification, financial.* B. *The marketing and* *announcement of the business.* C. *The grand opening of the business.* Using this evolution assign each major step a date.

Fill in the blanks. Now take an in-depth look at what is needed to get to point A, from point A to point B, etc. Write these steps down in specific detail and assign each a date.

The basic template construction of your goal is complete. Type this up, print it out, and keep a

> I have found when it's time to make decisions, it's easy to get confused when listening to everyone's advice. Spend some time reflecting by yourself and do what is best for you. Remember, it has to work for you. Do what you believe you need to do. Just think of the kids.
>
> *Charlotte Smith*
> *Enfield, Connecticut*

copy in your planner. Check your progress against this goal regularly. If you get off track, don't give up, just sit down and retrace your steps, adjusting the plan as necessary.

TEN STEPS TO A MORE MANAGED LIFE

If you have completed the preceding exercise, you should have a simple evaluation of where you are and where you hope to be. You have used the goal identifying method to make a map for each of your priorities. Now we're ready to put it all together with ten simple steps to create a life-management system.

Learning to successfully plan your time and follow the plan is the most important key to structuring your single-parent household. But many people resist the idea of tracking their time. Maybe it seems like just "another thing to do" in an already harried schedule. I urge people who feel this way to try this system for one month. I tell them that if it doesn't work, pitch it. Most single parents I have worked with are willing to make the one month commitment, and over 90% continue to use the system.

Let's get started with your own system to take control of your life and your time. As you glance through this section, you might be tempted to skip a step or two. I caution you that this is like a recipe.

Skipping one step is the equivalent of leaving out an ingredient. For maximum success use *all* the ingredients.

STEP ONE: TAKE STOCK OF HOW YOU CURRENTLY USE YOUR TIME.

Perhaps the most tedious of all the steps is to figure out exactly where your time is currently going. The balance wheel provided an overview of where you are. If possible, try to get even more specific. Many time management experts suggest carrying a planner and writing down everything you do for a week in fifteen minute increments. I personally wouldn't recommend it because I could never find the time to do it, and each time I tried, I lasted about an hour. What worked for me was to divide a piece of paper into the following increments: *Before Work, Morning at Work, Lunch Hour, Afternoon at Work, Evening With Samantha, After Samantha goes to bed.* In each square I wrote a few brief notes as to how I spent this time. I was able to keep up this method for the full week to get an accurate inventory of how I spent my time. Whatever method works for you is great, just try to gather some sort of weekly summary.

STEP TWO: EVALUATE YOUR WEEK, SIMPLIFY EXPECTATIONS AND IDENTIFY COMMON TIME WASTERS.

Recording a week's worth of activity can be an eye opener for many. In the hustle and bustle of life we often overlook how much time slips away that could be better utilized. As you look at your week, ask yourself the following:

How much time is spent spinning your wheels? Could positive planning help free up this time?

How many times do you make the same trip twice? (i.e. running errands in the same area of town, going to the store more than once.) How much time could positive planning free up if these trips were consolidated?

How much time is spent doing extra-commitments? (Helping church, school, friends or organizations.) If you budgeted a comfortable amount of time each week to others, but made a promise not to exceed it, would that help balance your life?

Do you really have to do everything? What on your list could be delegated or become a shared responsibility? Are there any items kids could help with? Could you pay a baby sitter a little extra to help clean or grocery shop? Could you start a car pool with other single parents to eliminate the constant demand of driving?

Do you have to do everything *so* often? If you are cleaning your home once a week, top to bottom, could that be done once a month and spot cleaning be done

> Single parenting can be one of the best or worst experiences you can have. It's up to you to make the most out of the situation.
>
> *Starr Clifton*
> *Martin, Tennessee*

weekly? Watch where your time is going. If it's being devoured by items that are low or nonexistent on your balance wheel, consider deleting or simplifying those tasks. Could you go to the grocery store monthly for the bulk of your food and just drop in weekly for perishables? If financial considerations prevent monthly trips to the grocery store, consider making this a goal to work toward.

What areas are simply getting too much time? Are the mornings devoted to too much dawdling and not enough doing? Are phone calls taking away from work time or family time?

What about you? Often the first thing to be eliminated from a schedule is time for one's self. How much time did you devote to yourself last week—without children? Did you take a walk alone? Relax for a while in peace and quiet? If you know that you aren't making time for adequate rejuvenation, sleep, exercise, diet or other self-maintenance, make this a starred priority. You need energy and self-care in order to nurture your children. Try and block out at least two hours a week for time that is completely devoted to you. The energy that you collect from two hours of focused time will easily recover those hours and more.

STEP THREE: MAKE AN INVENTORY
OF RESPONSIBILITIES AND GOALS

As you went through Step Two, you most likely pinpointed where your time is escaping and remedies for correcting it. You also probably figured out what tasks need to be done and what is done more out of habit than need. Step Three involves listing out all your responsibilities and goals. Once we have them all on the table, we can begin to insert them into your life management system.

> Make your priorities *yours*, not societies' friends' or family's.
>
> *Julie McKay*
> *Glover, Vermont*

On a fresh sheet of note paper list all the responsibilities you can think of. You may want to divide these into three columns—personal, family and work. The weekly inventory from Step One offers a good starting point of responsibilities. Keep this list handy, since more responsibilities may occur to you throughout the upcoming days.

Here are some responsibilities that may be on your list:

Car pool	*Finances*	*Grocery Shopping*
Vacuuming	*Cooking*	*Helping at School*
Education	*Exercise*	*Sweeping & Mopping*
Yard Work	*Pet Care*	*Church/Temple (or Synagogue)*
Volunteer Work	*Work*	*Laundry*

STEP FOUR: PRIORITIZE WITH
THE A, B, C METHOD

People have a tendency to create to-do lists and give each task equal billing. Most of the time, not everything needs to be done immediately. Listing everything together can create a false sense of urgency and unneeded stress.

Try identifying each item with a priority tag as shown here.

A - For items that must be done out of prior commitment or because they are part of your goals, priorities or value system.

B - For items that you hope to get done if you can complete all of the A-Priority tasks.

C - For items that need to be done at some point.

Many single parents find that when starting to prioritize, they have mostly A's and few B or C items. Since many of us don't practice regular planning, this is quite common. After a few weeks of planning and maximizing your time, you should begin to see a better balance of A, B, and C items.

Once each item is prioritized, compare your list to your balance wheel. Are you heading in the direction you want your life to take? Many people find that just recording these items on paper leads toward a more balanced wheel. If it doesn't for you, look over the list again. Is there anything else you could change or do to take you one step closer to your balanced goal?

STEP FIVE: CREATE A MONTHLY PLAN

A monthly plan is similar to a balance wheel in that it serves as an overview for where you are. Sketch in responsibilities and appointments on a monthly calendar. (More on monthly planners for families can be found in the *Communication Central* section of the *Managing The Single Parent Household* chapter.)

> Learn to let go of the things that don't really matter and spend that time with your children.
> *Carol Lopez*
> *Lexington, Kentucky*

As you write each item on your calendar, ask yourself—Does this coincide with the plan I have for my life? If not, why am I doing it? Sometimes these are items that we must do, but other times they might be things we do out of habit. For example, one woman, Cindy, reported that she cleaned her house thoroughly every Sunday and wished she could hire a maid. With her high devotion to cleaning, I asked her if this was a priority in her life. She replied that it wasn't.

After a few moments she said that her mother had always kept a very tidy house, and she felt that was part of her "expectations." Cindy switched from a thorough cleaning once a week to a monthly thorough cleaning and touch-ups on weekends. This created close to fourteen extra hours for her each month.

STEP SIX: CREATE A WEEKLY PLAN

The weekly plan sheet will serve as your primary tool for life management. I find that filling out a weekly plan sheet each Sunday afternoon or evening makes my weeks much more effective and helps to maximize each day. Here's how it works:

Each Sunday look at your responsibility list and your monthly calendar. Jot down any appointments or commitments on your weekly planner. Next, look at the time you have left and get out your balance wheels. Look at the ideal wheel you made earlier in this chapter. Glance at your goals. Fill in the remaining spaces with those items. Your schedule might be so hectic that you only see a few 30 minute increments over the course of the week. Don't let them slip away!

STEP SEVEN: CREATE A DAILY PLAN EACH NIGHT

Each night before retiring, jot down a plan for the following day. I find that using the same increment schedule I mentioned for tracking time works best for me. I simply divide a piece of paper into *morning responsibilities*, *afternoon responsibilities* and *evening responsibilities*. Others report great success with a system documented by hours. Find a method that works for you and you'll see how the daily plan accomplishes several vital functions:

(1) You don't have to "store" everything in your mind. You can jot it down, plan it and then let it go. This helps to alleviate stress.

(2) You can eliminate spinning your wheels and wondering what to do next since you simply follow the plan.

(3) It offers a sense of accomplishment as you mark off each item you have accomplished.

NOTE: On the top of your daily list you may want to name your top three priorities for the day. These tasks should contain three things that no matter what, would allow you to feel good about your day if you accomplished them.

STEP EIGHT: UTILIZE TO-DO LISTS

To-do lists offer a great release. I keep a notepad in my purse at all times. I use this to jot down anything I think of that I need to do. At one point, I tried to have just a master list at home, but soon noticed that I never thought of anything that needed to be done until I was stuck in traffic, playing at the park or at some other location equally far from my pen and paper.

By jotting down these items as they occur to you, a person doesn't have to continually focus on them, be preoccupied or try to remember them.

STEP NINE: ORGANIZE A
TIME MANAGEMENT CENTER

You will need to have a time-management center to keep track of your progress and schedules. If you don't have a spare drawer, pick up an accordion file at your local office supply store. Stock your file with the following:

- Scratch paper or to-do list paper
- A monthly calendar
- Pencils/Pens
- Weekly and daily calendars (Check into the many planners available today. There are several that can be customized to fit your needs. Or, if you have a computer, make your own forms, hole-punch them, and insert these papers into a three-ring binder. This allows you to customize your entire organizer.)
- A section to hold bills (folders that are three-hole-punched are excellent if you are using a three-ring binder)

- A section to hold important papers
- A section for receipts and other important items
- Stamps and assorted sized envelopes
- Note cards
- Frequently dialed numbers, doctor, etc.

> De-cluttering your life will give you lots of extra time with your kids. Throw out (or give away) everything not used. Get rid of negative people and surround yourself with positive people.
>
> *Maria C. Kleinbub*
> *Maspeth, New York*

- A list of immunizations for small children or other important medical records

STEP TEN: EVALUATE YOUR PROGRESS WEEKLY OR MONTHLY

Sit down with your balance wheel, goals and schedules on a regular basis. Make a new balance wheel based on what you have done over the last month or week. Are you getting closer to your goals? If so, continue on the same track. If not, double back and look for steps you may have skipped in the process.

SIMPLIFY YOUR LIFE

Have you ever felt controlled by life's external circumstances and responsibilitiies? Do you ever feel there is so much stuff in your house that you'll never get organized? Do paperwork, finances, budgeting and bills loom? Does time seem like a hard to find commodity? Are your days so filled with commitments that they blend one into another?

If so, you're not alone. Millions of Americans are suffering from today's demanding lifestyles. And more and more people are joining a new trend. The trend of simplifying one's life. Overcommitment and overburden lead to stress, frustration and a sense of being "out of control."

The following tips can help you narrow-in on the clutter chaos and create a more calming life.

The closet. Start by visiting your grocery store and bringing home a few big boxes. These are your garage sale or donation boxes. Start with your closet. Most of us have more than we can possibly wear or clothes that haven't been worn because we don't feel comfortable or confident in them. All of those can go. Donate them, or have a rummage sale and use the proceeds to buy a few pieces you *will* wear.

Do you need more than one? How many books do you have right now that you have been meaning to read? How many books can you read at one time? If you have stacks of unread books you are only adding clutter to your life. You may also be wasting money if, by the time you are ready to read those books, your interests change and there is a new book you would rather read. Simplifying is all about one thing at a time.

Tackling the Stuff. George Carlin once said, "Think of it. That's all your house is. It's a place to keep your stuff. If you didn't have so much stuff, you wouldn't need a house. That's all your house is. A pile of stuff with a cover on it. It's a place to keep your stuff while you go out and get more stuff!"

As you look at all the stuff in your home, remember this formula—stuff equals stress. The more stuff you have, the more you have to maintain, clean and repair. The basic key to simplifying your life is to simplify your stuff.

Think of everything you do in terms of priorities. What are your priorities in life? Do you long to have more time with your children? Is there an unfulfilled dream you would like to

> Decide what is most important to the well-being of you and your children (secure home, time together, job) and get rid of everything else (feeling that you have to be room mother, scout leader, extended family care-taker). Though I might like to do those things I once did, by giving them up I find I have much more time and energy to devote to my kids, my job, my home and myself.
>
> *Single Mother*
> *Denver, Colorado*

pursue? Identify your top few priorities and then observe how your actions affect them.

For example, if your top priority is spending time with your children, does buying a new outfit achieve that? If you have a comparable outfit, could that money be better spent?

Cutting Down. Simplifying isn't about being frugal. It's about deciding what is important to you and what makes you feel better about yourself and your life. It's about doing more of the things that make you feel good—by cutting out the things that don't offer as much gratification.

Take the following situation. Let's say you grab a cup of coffee every day on your way to work. It's become a ritual. Do you get excited as you pull up to that drive-through? Probably not. You might glance at your watch and think, *I wish they would hurry up. I need my coffee and I still have to get through rush hour.* What if you brewed coffee at home, but, to start off your week on Monday mornings, you treated yourself to meeting a friend for a coffee? Which would give you more gratification? Which would simplify and enhance your life?

Same with dinner. If you bring home fast food on a regular basis, why not make it just a couple of times each month—but make it more special by taking the kids for an extra hour in the playland?

Trap of the free item. I was amazed when I looked around my office at how many things I had collected just because they were free. Newspapers, brochures, catalogs—enough to wallpaper my office twice.

As I looked through the items, a few were valuable, but most just took up space and took extra time to organize and weed through. (Not to mention that it certainly was not environmentally friendly for me to take items that I wouldn't use.) Now, when I see something free, I think twice and don't take it unless it's something I'm positive I'll use.

A CRASH COURSE IN SIMPLIFICATION

- "Use it or lose it" is the golden rule of simplifying one's life.

- If you can't figure out what a gizmo or gadget does, then all it's doing is taking up space.

- Take ten minutes every night to un-clutter. Have a race with your kids to put everything away. If you do this nightly as part of your bedtime routine you avoid the danger of letting your house get "out of control."

- Tackle one project at a time. Whether the project is cleaning, organizing, reading a book or working on a craft project, finish each project completely before purchasing or starting another.

- Limit junk drawers to one in your entire home.

- Teach "the art of simplicity" to your kids.

- If you don't have a place to put something, don't buy it. Avoid making space for more clutter.

- Don't keep catalogs. They are not only clutter-building, they are a temptation to spend money.

- Donate your books to the local library when you are finished with them. (Ask for a receipt as the donation may be tax-deductible.)

- Don't become obsessed with saving everything for a later use. How many plastic and paper bags does one person need?

- When you are organizing and come across something you kind of like, but don't really use, try to think of someone who not only likes the item, but also will use it. Make that person's day by giving it to them.

- Every couple of months tackle the sock drawer. If there isn't a match now, there probably won't be one later. Toss solo socks or make sock puppets with your kids for some inexpensive family entertainment.

- Don't waste time looking for warranties, manuals or important receipts. Create a special drawer where only these things are kept. Using a drawer eliminates the chance of the papers never making it to a file or being misfiled.

- Bill systems. Try the following for a quick way to manage your incoming mail and bills. Purchase three magnetic envelope size holders. Place these on the side of your refrigerator. Use the top one for bills you need to pay with your first paycheck each month. Use the second for the bills that come out of your second paycheck. The third is for all outgoing mail and a roll of stamps. When you pick up your mail each day, sort it right by the bill-holders. Throw out envelopes, special offers and all the clutter that comes with bills these days. When it comes time to pay your bills, remove the top holder and find a quiet place to do your paper-work. Then return that holder below the other one and make it for your next paycheck.

TWENTY-MINUTE SANITY SAVERS

Twenty minutes for your-self is one of the best stress-management tactics in the world. Moments to fantasize, dream, collect your thoughts, or dive into a another world can give a person the energy needed to face a day. As you devise your new, more scheduled lifestyle, make sure to include breaks for your own sanity-savers.

> Don't give up. It's a struggle from start to finish, but you'll come out of it a much stronger and more confi-dent person than you ever were. People always say to me, "I don't know how you do it," or "I couldn't do it." Well, I don't have a choice in the matter. I keep plugging along. But after seven years, I'm seeing the light at the end of the tunnel and all the hard work is starting to pay off.
>
> *Lisa Angstadt, 29*
> *Single mom of two children*
> *Phoenix, Arizona*

Begin the day with peace of mind. Set your alarm twenty minutes earlier than your typical setting. It's not important to wake up and get your day started at this point. Instead, take twenty minutes to think through your day. Imagine what you hope to accomplish and visualize yourself working through your agenda with confidence, joy and ease. Think positive statements about your life, your family and yourself. This allows you to make a dry run of your day and to start each morn-ing feeling confident and ready instead of frustrated, rushed and behind. Try this every day for a week. The rewards will be so great that it will become easy to adapt this time-saver into a ritual.

End your day with a pep talk. If morning is your worst hour, adapt the above to a nighttime ritual. Before fading into sleep, have a seat in a comfortable chair (to avoid falling asleep) and recount the positives of your day. Close your eyes and imagine watching yourself in the context of the upcoming day. See yourself handling everything smoothly and confidently.

> Do the best you can do in all aspects of your life and let the rest go.
> *Single Mother*
> *Lake Tahoe, Nevada*

Take a break. If you typically spend your lunch hour running errands, meeting others' needs or eating with co-workers, try a variation once or twice a week. Pack a brown bag lunch and a good book and find a spot to curl up and read. Or just relax and take a walk. The important thing is to clear your mind and spend your time thinking about your goals, dreams and what is important to you.

Take a time-out. Every evening insist on a time-out in your family's nightly schedule. Choose a half-hour that is time for *you*. Don't choose something so late that you will be tempted to go to sleep. 9:00 to 9:30 works well for many single parents. If you have older children who are usually awake, ask them to spend this time in their rooms or in a different section of your home. Use this time to focus on something you enjoy.

THE JOYS OF A DISCOVERY PROGRAM

After the day-in and day-out ritual of schedules and demands, life can sometimes take on a monotonous tone that leads to boredom, frustration or depression. A discovery program is the perfect cure.

Take a set of index cards and write things you've always wanted to do, but not made time for. One single father's list looked like this:

- Learn how to scuba dive.
- Take an overnight hike in the Cascades.

- Spend a day making a photo essay of my children and family.
- Writing a book on the local culture.
- Enjoy an afternoon movie—alone.

You get the idea. Take these cards and paper clip them into your planner using the extra time you created in your week to accomplish them.

A fun variation is to choose discoveries that fit into the two hour time slots we devised in Step Two. Jot down ten or so, and then each week pick one at random to enjoy. The key is rediscovering all the newness offered by life, all the excitement and things awaiting our discovery—when we only choose to make the time to live. This is also a great activity to do with children. Sit around a table and brainstorm ideas for the index cards and then aim to do one activity every week or biweekly.

Take a moment to allot a few blocks of time for yourself, your needs and your goals. Consider taking a personal day at work, if possible, to get yourself on track, organized and rejuvenated. You deserve it.

Making time takes time. But this is one of the most valuable ways to spend time. Don't let life slip away when you aren't looking. Plan to live—to make the most of each day and your potential.

> Take time out for yourself when you begin to feel crushed by the enormous physical, emotional and financial responsibilities of doing it all yourself. Lock yourself in the bathroom with a hot bath. Get a sitter and go to the gym. Put the kids to bed early. Take a few moments to feel better about you.
>
> *Single Mother*
> *Charlotte, North Carolina*

MORE WORDS OF WISDOM
ON NAVIGATING THE SINGLE-PARENT LIFE

"Make time for yourself or your insanity will impact the children. Your children are learning how to maintain their own mental health from you. It's okay for them to see you lose your mind, temper or credit cards, as long as they also see you take steps to recover from the problem."

> *Tracy Brant*
> *Reading, Pennsylvania*

"Don't second-guess yourself so much. Once a decision is made, it is in the past."

> *Diana Williams*
> *Norcross, Georgia*

"Remember that your life and the life of your child(ren) did not end with your divorce."

> *Single Father*
> *Tampa, Florida*

"Take it one day at a time. Forgive yourself for being a less than perfect parent, learn from these times and do better the next time."

> *D. M.*
> *California*

"Be positive about the situation, even when it isn't a positive one."

> *Gerrie C. Gray*
> *Falls Church, Virginia*

"Sometimes it's hard being a single parent and making ALL the decisions, but I have educated myself about parenting and continue to do so. I read, read, read, constantly. I read all the books and magazines I can get my hands on."

> *Single Mother*
> *Portland, Oregon*

"Downsize both your house and your outside activities."

> *Single Mother*
> *Texas*

"Don't forget about yourself. You are the most important person in this family. Without you, your children will suffer—so make sure you give yourself time to nurture you."

> *Single Mother*
> *Canada*

"Get plenty of interests that don't center around your child (even if you take them with you—as I do), remembering to be a person as well as a parent!"

> *Single Mother*
> *Las Vegas, Nevada*

RESOURCES FOR NAVIGATING THE SINGLE-PARENT LIFE

"YMCAs collectively are the country's largest not-for-profit human service organization, serving 14.8 million girls, boys, women and men nationwide. Each YMCA is community based and makes its own programming decisions to meet local needs. In its own way, every YMCA works to build strong kids, strong families and strong communities. Contact your local YMCA for specific programs and offerings in your area. To locate a YMCA near you visit the *Find Your Y* feature at the YMCA's web site *http://www.ymca.net*"

Putting Fun Into Your Family Life
courtesy of the YMCA of the USA

Today's families are busier than ever. Everyone's got an agenda to follow, from baby on up. Despite the hectic pace, it's important for families to make an effort to have fun together. Happiness is an important life skill that doesn't just happen. It may sound funny, but you have to work at it.

Listed below are ways in which you can add fun to your family's life.

Make ordinary things fun. Happiness is a way of looking at life. Turn everyday experiences into lighthearted fun. Make up silly names for each other or change the words to songs as you drive somewhere. Play games while grocery shopping as you head up and down the aisles. Put on some music and dance around after dinner. Wash the car together and then turn it into a splash party.

Get in the habit of savoring the moment. Learn to live in the present. Don't get bogged down with analyzing a situation or lecturing for the sake of teaching. Just take it all in with your senses—observe and enjoy.

Take plenty of strolls down memory lane. Talk about the good times you've had in the past and help build your child's memories. Take pictures and collect souvenirs. Kids love it when you tell them about themselves—when they were born, what their first words were, when they learned to walk, etc.

Encourage your child's playful side. Help your child develop a sense of humor. Teach him how to find joy in life and not take it too seriously. Laugh at his jokes, then make up some of your own.

Be playful yourself. Children enjoy themselves most when they're around parents who are playful. They learn how to keep things in perspective when they see mom or dad act silly at times. If you don't take yourself too seriously, you'll be more human in your child's eyes.

Eleven fun ideas:

- Keep scrapbooks or photo albums of family activities.
- Keep a book of family quotations. Your children say some hilarious things you won't want to forget. Write them down in a bound book, then read it together at some time.
- Make the first Saturday of every month Weird Breakfast Day. Serve something unusual like pizza or Chinese food. On the flip side, give the kids scrambled eggs, waffles, or pancakes for dinner every now and then. They'll love it!
- Have squirt-gun free-for-alls in warm weather, pillow fights in cold weather.
- Hold a story night with older children in which everyone tells part of a story, making it as silly as possible.
- Rent silly movies, pop some popcorn, and sit around and laugh together.
- Jump into a pile of leaves.
- Get a box of colored chalk and decorate the sidewalk together.
- Turn the music up, roll back the rugs and dance!

- Do seasonal things like picking apples in the fall or taking a trip to a lake in the summer.
- Let the housework go for once. Get out of the house and play!

"YWCA of the USA is committed to the empowerment of women and girls and the elimination of racism." You can request their annual report and newsletter by writing to YWCA of the USA, Empire State Building, 350 Fifth Avenue, Suite 301, New York, NY 10118. Or visit their web site at *http://www.ywca.org.*

FOR FURTHER READING ON A SIMPLER LIFESTYLE

Simple Abundance: A Daybook of Comfort and Joy, by Sara Ban Breathnach (Warner Books). This bestselling title is an incredible resource to remind us of all of the beauty in life and how to make the most of each day.

FOR FURTHER READING ON TIME MANAGEMENT

First Things First, by Stephen Covey, A. Roger Merrill, and Rebecca R. Merril (Simon & Schuster). This book goes far beyond the basics. It offers a complete look at the paradigms of life and how we can successfully manage our priorities.

The Working Woman's Guide To Managing Time: Take Charge of Your Job and Your Life While Taking Care of Yourself, by Roberta Roesch (Prentice Hall). A practical guidebook with easy to implement strategies and hundreds of great ideas.

The Idiot's Guide to Organizing Your Life, by Georgene Lockwood, (Alpha books). A lighthearted, often humorous guide to the basics of managing time, space, paperwork and streamlining one's life.

SHARED LIVING RESOURCE CENTER (SLRC)

"SLRC is a community that benefits single-parent and two-parent families by sharing land and buildings, costs, resources, child-care, common amenities and decision making." They provide an information packet that includes an SLRC general brochure, list of services, workshop flyer, book reviews, articles and more. The cost is $3.00 and that includes shipping and handling. Write to the Shared Living Resource Center, 2337 Parker St. #9, Berkeley, CA 94704-2841.

Current Balance Wheel

Using the categories below,
draw how your life is balanced today.
See page 34 for an example

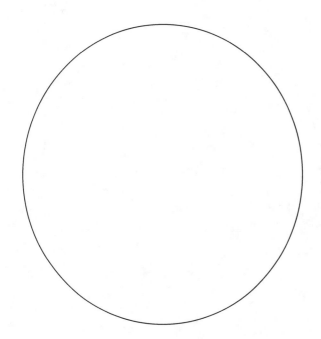

- Spirituality
- Emotional Well-being
- Family
- Physical Health
- Relationships
- Career

Ideal Balance Wheel

Using the categories below,
draw how your life would be balanced ideally.
See page 35 for an example

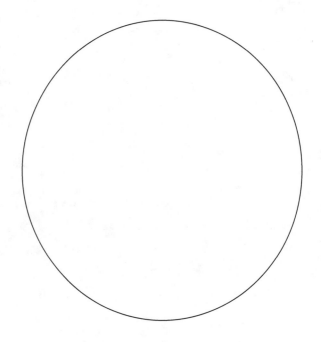

- Spirituality
- Emotional Well-being
- Family
- Physical Health
- Relationships
- Career

Daily Schedule

Before Work	
Morning Hours	
Lunch Hour	
Afternoon Hours	
Evening	
After Kids Go To Bed	
Top Three Priorities for today	

CHAPTER THREE
MANAGING THE SINGLE-PARENT HOUSEHOLD

"I never feel I'm doing enough."

"I want to spend more time with my kids—I just can't find the time or am too tired when it finally arrives!"

"I feel like I'm always working on something but never getting caught up."

"I'm always behind the eight-ball."

"I don't feel our family has enough quality time together."

"I feel like I'm being pulled in several directions."

"I frequently feel stressed out or overwhelmed."

How many of the statements above can you relate to? If even one sounds familiar, learning to better manage the single-parent household may be your key to alleviating stressors and creating a smoother, more enjoyable life.

COMMUNICATION CENTRAL

Schedules and time management systems are the quickest and easiest ways to eliminate conflict and better manage your household. It's amazing how wonderful these tools are and how they simplify one's life, but it's even more amazing that with all these benefits, few people use them! It will take a few hours to set up your system, but it's worth it.

Communication Central will become an important place in your home. To begin, mount a weekly and monthly dry-erase calendar on your refrigerator. Assign each of your children a colored marker. Let them be responsible for recording their school notes, field trips, report deadlines, etc. on the calendar. Parents should have two colors. One for your personal schedule and another for family events and other activities that concern the family as a whole.

Other necessities for Communication Central include:

An address book to keep all phone numbers handy. On the first page, fill in emergency contact numbers and make sure that your children know how to access, and when to use, these numbers.

Keep a message book by the phone, and teach children how to properly take messages. Spiral message notebooks tend to work better than the notepads since the messages stay in one spot.

Use your bulletin board to leave each other notes or reminders. Have some fun and leave each other special notes on special papers. A little gesture like this can brighten the day of both parent and child. You may also want to supply hooks for each family member to store their keys.

Create a weekly calendar of meals, and plan these out in

> COMMUNICATION
> CENTRAL
> SHOPPING LIST
>
> A weekly planner
> A set of colored dry-erase
>   markers
> Dry-erase calendars (both
>   monthly and weekly)
> Address book
> A small bulletin board
> Notepad
> Two letter trays
> A message book (spiral
>   notebooks work fine)
> Scrap paper and tacks
> A three-ring binder and
>   assorted color
>   construction paper
> Hole punch

advance. A Sunday afternoon is a good day to sit down and have a small family meeting so everyone can touch base. Create the upcoming dinner schedule during this time and a shopping list. Post it on the refrigerator for easy reference.

Create a kid's phone book. Purchase some construction paper and a three-ring-binder. Let each child have their own color paper, i.e. Kim's Red Pages, John's Purple Pages, etc. Punch the paper and insert it into the binder. Kids can record frequently dialed numbers, schedules and notes in their pages. You may want to tie a string to a binder ring and attach it to a table near the phone to prevent it from "walking" away.

Lastly, put an "In" & "Out" basket somewhere within your child's reach. Anything she needs your help with or signature on can go in the "In" basket. You can also use this for items you need to read, file or respond to. Once completed place the item in the "Out" basket. Once a week go through the Out basket and handle each item to avoid pile up.

EMERGENCY!

With only one adult in the household, it's even more important that children know what to do and how to handle emergencies, since, if you're occupied, they'll need to think fast. Setting up an emergency system and performing a few dry-runs is a precaution every single parent should take.

Begin with a laminated list of phone numbers mounted near each phone. Make sure to print or type the list in large legible letters. In a time of panic, this makes it easier to read. Check the first few pages of your phone book for important numbers and add them to your own family and emergency contacts. At the bottom of the sheet write pertinent information you or your child may need to know in the event of emergency—blood type, allergies to medicines, home address, fire and police numbers, etc. Teach children when to use each number. Practice by unplugging the phone and letting your child dial and recite the information. Or let him call a family member or adult friend to practice.

Have fire evacuation plans for each room of the house as well as other precautions for your region (what to do in the event of tornado, earthquake, etc.). Practice these at least twice each year. At each practice session check all related materials, i.e., smoke detectors, fire extinguishers.

Stock your house with first-aid supplies. Many pharmacies carry plastic kits including all the basic supplies. Consider purchasing one of these for each floor of your house. (It never hurts to have one in the car, too.) Other items you may want to add to the first-aid kit:

Ammonia*	Alcohol*	Eye dropper
Ipecac (to induce vomiting)*	Iodine*	Scissors*
Tweezers*	Thermometer*	

Keep these items out of reach of young children.

You may also want to consider taking a first-aid class with your child if he or she is old enough, or taking one on your own. I took an Infant CPR class prior to my daughter's birth and learned that one out of three children is injured each year. A first-aid class contains life skills that you and your child will be able to put to use probably more times than any of us would like.

SANITY SAVING FAMILY MEETINGS

A family meeting is the perfect venue for all family members to touch base and work together in creating a well-run household. Once a week (biweekly if your schedules are really jammed), request everyone's presence for a meeting.

In interviewing single parents on what makes a successful meeting, I put together the following template. Adjust this to meet your own needs.

FAMILY MEETING AGENDA

- Get oriented. Begin with each family member having 2-5 minutes to update everyone on his or her week.

- Using a weekly calendar have each family member announce his or her weekly commitments and record them on a calendar.

- Discuss any upcoming family events, visitation changes, or other variations to your schedule.

- Check progress on chore and reward systems.

- Discuss any issues or problems between siblings.

- Let each child bring up any concerns or questions he or she has.

- Plan the weekly menu together.

- Choose a fun, family activity for the upcoming week.

- Adjourn.

> Prioritize what is important to you and your family and don't worry if there is not always time to get everything else done.
>   *Erica Bodner*
>   *Westlake Village, California*

THE NEW HOUSE RULES

Your first family meeting offers the perfect time to post the new house rules. It's a reality that with the changing of family form comes the changing of responsibility. Take a moment to think through ways to improve your lifestyle and home management without inconveniencing other family members. List these ideas on an 11x17 sheet of paper and post them on the refrigerator. Here are a few ideas to get you started:

- Each person will set aside two or three hours during the week for a meeting and to help around the house.

- Next day preparations. Each person is responsible for packing any needed materials (lunch, backpack, etc.) for the next day.

- Each person will jot down their commitments on the Communication Central board.

- Each person will put their own items away each night.

- Each person will sort and hang their own laundry.

Ignore the temptation to request everything be done your way or the spirit of teamwork will quickly backfire. Recognize that by delegating tasks they will be done differently and probably not how you would do them yourself. But the benefit of teamwork should outweigh a less-than-perfect job.

CHORE AND REWARD SYSTEMS

Chore and reward systems are one of the most important keys for managing the single-parent household. A good system can inspire children while teaching them responsibility and discipline—not to mention easing your own commitments.

The basics. A chore and reward system is a visual tool that lets children perform household tasks in order to earn something they would really like.

Make a list of what you need help with. If you had it your way, what would you delegate around the house? Perhaps cooking or cleaning up after dinner? Does laundry or dusting make you cringe? What about taking out garbage or mowing the lawn? Write down any responsibilities you'd like to delegate that are age-appropriate for your children.

Next, ask your children to tell you something they would really, really like. Find a picture of this item and place it on a piece of construction paper. Using your list of tasks, create a "road" that leads to the item. As they complete each task, initial it, and once they work through the road they get their requested item.

> Straighten up only the public areas of your place—don't worry about the messes behind closed doors!
> *Shelly Weiner*
> *Henderson, Nevada*

CHORE AND REWARD SYSTEMS WITH TODDLERS

Chore and reward systems can work with children as young as two! True they won't be very efficient at vacuuming but there are ways they can help make the days go smoother.

I used a system with my daughter that models the above. Using a piece of construction paper I made twenty 1x1 inch squares. At the bottom I made one large square and put a picture of an Elmo helium balloon. Each time she cleaned up her toys, was a good listener for the day, got dressed without a fight, went to sleep without a fight or went to the bathroom "on the potty," I let her choose a sticker to place on a square. (The stickers were all her favorite characters and animals, dinosaurs, Barney, butterflies, etc.)

> Find a comfortable routine and stick to it.
> *Matthew H. Strope*
> *Cornelia, Georgia*

When the sheet was full, we made a special adventure out of purchasing her balloon. We went to the store and bought only the balloon, taking great care to pick one out.

TIME FOR EVERYONE

When talking to children from single-parent families, those who were most satisfied were children who received one-on-one time with their parents. This didn't mean they had to have a day-long outing but "just sit around and hang," as fourteen-year-old Laura put it.

When considering running your household, don't forget to schedule in one-on-one time with each child as frequently as possible. Some families report success with ten minutes a day while others prefer an afternoon biweekly. Try different options and see what works best for you and your children.

THE IMPORTANCE OF TRADITION

Unfortunately when a family changes form, many of the traditions that were once shared bring a sense of sadness instead of a sense of pleasure. Instead of continuing with traditions that stir painful memories or avoiding traditions, adapt new traditions for your new family form. Brainstorm with your children and let them offer ideas for traditions they've always longed for. See how outrageous you can get. Have fun with it.

WHAT'S FOR DINNER?
AND OTHER KITCHEN HASSLES

Food preparation is a responsibility that many single parents yearn to simplify. With over an hour a day spent in the kitchen, parents seek easy ways to get in and out of the kitchen fast—leaving more time to spend with children.

Once-a-month-cooking is a great idea for a family event while also cutting down on your kitchen hours each week. The theory is that you buy in bulk (thus saving money) and spend one day cooking for many days worth of meals.

It's also the perfect way to avoid the "What's For Dinner" syndrome that causes many-a-parent to glance through the cupboard and dial for a pizza out of exhaustion.

> Give the kids your personal time. To quote my favorite refrigerator magnet, "Cleaning the house while the kids are still growing is like shoveling the walk while it's still snowing!"
>
> *Jodi F.*
> *Maplewood, Minnesota*

Deborah Taylor-Hough has mastered the Once-A-Month Cooking method and shares her wisdom in this excerpt.

A DAY IN THE LIFE
OF ONCE-A-MONTH COOKING
by Deborah Taylor-Hough

Well, I've stared at my empty freezer long enough. Tonight I'll sit down, plan my month's menus and make out a shopping list for tomorrow morning. Then Saturday will be cooking day. It takes me about six hours of one day to complete my Once A Month Cooking (OAMC.) A long day of cooking, true, but having a home cooked meal available every day for a month, with no more fuss than just the preparation of a side dish and a salad is heaven!

A friend suggested OAMC. My initial response was, "I'd love to try that, but we don't have a separate freezer. Just the little one over the fridge. I don't have enough room to store a month's worth of meals." Well, my friend encouraged me to start small, doing Twice-a-Month Cooking, packing the meals in freezer bags for more compact stacking in the freezer. I figured, "What have I got to lose?" So, I rolled up my sleeves and gave it a try.

Those two weeks were wonderful!

I've also found that buying in bulk for these big cooking days can easily save enough money to pay for a good used freezer. Check your newspaper ads. You never know what kind of deals you might come across. Ask friends, relatives and neighbors to let you know if they hear of anyone moving out of state, or remodeling his or her kitchen. I've known folks who have gotten freezers for free, just by making a few phone calls. You never know.

The first part of my OAMC is done: Menu planning—

This is what I'm going to make:
All-American BBQ Sandwiches (3 meals)
Broccoli Quiche (3 meals)
Baked Macaroni Casserole (4 meals)
Spaghetti (3 meals)
French Bread Pizza (2 meals)
Cheese Enchiladas (5 meals)
Cabbage Rolls (5 meals)
Island Fish Sauté (4 meals)
Creole Chicken (3 meals)
Broccoli Chicken (4 meals)
Scalloped Potatoes w/Ham (5 meals)

That's 41 meals stacked in my freezer by Saturday night!

There will also be about 4-5 meals (or more) of homemade vegetable chicken soup made from leftovers thrown into the chicken stock. I have a notebook that I use for OAMC. I don't use the Once-a-Month Cooking book anymore. I found their recipes too expensive for my limited grocery budget. I adapted the OAMC methods to my own recipes, and I've also collected recipes from other OAMC cooks I know.

My personal OAMC cookbook is a simple three-ring binder. I have filled it with plastic page protectors to slip in recipes, shopping lists and other OAMC related information. I'm always updating my notebook as I find new recipes and tips.

I have a particular meal plan that I often follow [Note: many of the recipes from this inexpensive meal plan were originally published and developed by Cheryl Lindsey in *Gentle Spirit Magazine* about five years ago.], but I adapt the plan to what I have on hand, or any specific requests that my family makes. A while ago I set up a Master Shopping List for my inexpensive 30 meal plan. I ran a bunch of photocopies, and I keep the shopping list in the first page of my notebook. When it's time to plan the menu and go shopping, I slip one of the Master Shopping Lists out of its page protector, and I'm ready to add to the list as needed. (This saves having to rethink my entire shopping list each time.)

The next page in my notebook is a list called "Order of Preparation of 30 Meals." I have everything pretty well laid out. What I need to cook the night before, what I need to do first, what order to prepare the meals, etc. Then I have the recipes I use most frequently in the next section of the notebook. I have a separate section for other recipes that have already been adapted to my way of OAMC, and then another section of just generic frequently used recipes that my family loves. Eventually, I will try to incorporate more of those recipes into my OAMC plans.

I'd like to have 4 or 5 different Master Lists. The list I usually use now is my Low-Cost version of OAMC. At times when money isn't quite so tight, I'd like to have other menu plans to choose from as well.

My shopping trip on Friday takes just over an hour. I do all of my shopping at one store since I'm always strapped for time when I shop. We only have one car, so my time at the store is very limited. I could probably save money if I shopped around for better prices at different stores, but my time and effort is worth money, too. The store I've chosen for my regular shopping is the one I've found to be generally cheaper all around than the other stores in town.

I now have over 40 meals in my freezer. Phew! What a relief to be done with it for another month. A friend of mine and I were talking about how that one big cooking day is sometimes so incredibly tiring. After the big cooking is done, you might ask yourself, "What did I do THAT for?" But about two days of eating ready-made, yummy meals, and you'll forget the labor that went into that freezer full of food. (Sort of like forgetting childbirth after you hold the baby.)

To purchase the ingredients for 40+ main dishes to feed our family of five (plus salad fixings, fruits, vegetables, shampoo, dish soap, paper products, milk, eggs, cereal, peanut butter, jelly, bread, etc.), I spent $166 grocery shopping on Friday. Not too shabby. I had taken $180 with me to the store, so after everything was said and done, I even had enough money left to buy myself a latte' and a U-Bake Pizza (large pepperoni for $5.99) for our dinner on shopping day. Nice treat!

Some of the items on my shopping list, I already had on hand. But I also needed to stock up on a few things I normally have, so I guess it all balances out.

If I had to purchase the items that I had on hand, it would have added $10 for the ground beef, about $3 for the turkey ham, $2 for the tomato sauce, and about $5 for the frozen veggies. So adding that to the $166 I spent on Friday, it would have been about $186.

When they bagged up my groceries, it was 14 shopping bags full. I almost always get amazed comments from the cashiers about how little my groceries cost. They tell me that usually when they see that amount of groceries, it's well over $250, if not closer to $300. What can I say?

I usually purchase store brands, unless I know for certain that my family doesn't like them. For example, I've tried making my yummy spaghetti sauce with jars of generic spaghetti sauce. That got a big thumbs down from everyone. Now I always purchase good quality sauce (Ragu, Prego, etc.). Usually one of the big brands is on sale, so I purchase that brand. My family can really tell the difference between cheap spaghetti sauce and most brands. With other items, they're not quite so picky. I try store brands, but if they don't go over well, I don't use them again.

Friday night, I cooked the chicken in a large pot, and put it in the fridge to cool overnight. I also made my spaghetti sauce (ended up with 4 meals' worth for spaghetti and 2 for pizza) on Friday, since it goes together so quickly.

This was my order of preparation on cooking day (more or less):
Debone, chop and boil chicken. Put broth in refrigerator.
Peel and mince onions.
Steam cabbage heads whole.
Grate carrots.
Chop peppers and celery.
Grate the cheese.
Cook millet.
Brown ground beef.
Cut ham into ½ inch cubes.
Prepare Cabbage Rolls.
Prepare Cheese Enchiladas.
Prepare Creole Chicken.
Prepare Island Fish Sauté.
Prepare Broccoli Chicken.
Prepare Broccoli Quiche.

Slice and cook potatoes.

Prepare Scalloped Potatoes w/Ham.

Prepare Baked Macaroni and Cheese.

Prepare All-American BBQ Sandwiches.

Use leftover veggies, meats, tomato sauce, noodles, etc. to make soup with the broth from cooking the chicken.

The total time spent cooking was about 7 hours including a break to eat lunch and an afternoon visit from friends.

I realized an added benefit of OAMC is I have more desire to cook other things during the week when I'm not so focused on getting that main dinner meal prepared each day. When I know I only have to warm something up, I tend to do more extra baking and special cooking. I really do love to cook, but the "daily-ness" of it wears thin after awhile. For me, OAMC restores the joy of cooking special things.

For more information on Debi's offerings, see the Simple Pleasures Press listing in the resource section of this chapter.

RECREATING THE FAMILY DINNER

With the day-to-day demands of current times, the once typical sit-down dinner has evaporated in many households. Yet, this period serves as a wonderful tie to cement families, touch base and share time. If the family dinner isn't possible in your household, try to designate another special sit-down meal. Some single parents report success with a Sunday brunch or a once-a-week all work-together, eat-together, clean-up-together meal. To entice kids to join in try something a little out of the usual such as theme dinners.

How theme dinners work:

- Choose something of interest to your child. This could be hobby-related, a place your child has traveled or something your child is studying in school.

- Find an applicable dinner menu. For example, if your child is into Cowboy themes, a good southwestern menu, some country music and a line-dancing video would do the trick.

- Dress for the occasion. Have each family member rig up appropriate attire.

- Live out the evening with the cuisine, ambiance and attire appropriate for the theme dinner.

Ideas for theme dinners:

- A Night In The Orient - Use chopsticks, sit on the floor and wear robes.

- On Vacation - Dress in tourist clothing and sample different types of cuisine.

- Classic Elegance - Prepare a fine dinner, dress in your best clothes and play classical music. (Young children have fun playing waiter or waitress.)

LIVE A WEEK IN A DAY

Delegating the day or afternoon during which you have the least commitments as an organizational day can help to get your family one step ahead for the upcoming week. On this day, conduct your family meeting and prepare for the week ahead. Here are some tasks to fill your day and don't forget to have kids help too!

- Plan the menu for the following week. Make a shopping list and go together. Try to choose at least one entree that you can prepare and freeze for two or three upcoming meals.

- Make a weekly schedule. Have each family member pencil in their commitments. From extracurricular activities to time with friends, record everything along with how kids will get from point A to point B. Make any arrangements needed to complete the schedule.

- Check wardrobes. Make sure each family member has the clothes needed for the upcoming week and that all buttons, hems, etc. are in place. Older children can be in charge of organizing this for themselves and letting you know if any item is in need of repair.

- Get the house prepared. If having a clean home is important to you, incorporate cleaning into your weekly planning day. Make a list of what you would like done to the house and divide the list between you and your children. When all is done, take a special adventure, such as mini-golf, a picnic or movie.

- Make a replenish list. Keep a shopping list on your refrigerator. As any item is emptied, write it on the list and have the kids do the same. Then each week grab this, and use it as your base grocery list.

- Keep some quick fixes in your home. Have a frozen pizza, macaroni and cheese, spaghetti or other quick fix meal for nights when time gets away from you. This alleviates the unhealthy pattern and money traps of opting for fast food.

SIMPLE WAYS TO INCREASE
DAY-TO-DAY QUALITY TIME

- Use your answering machine. When working with children on homework or eating dinner, let the answering machine take incoming calls.

- Combine duties. Instead of rushing children through bedtime schedules, use it as a time to catch up. Blow bubbles in the bathtub or read stories to help you both unwind and enjoy each other.

- If you pick up children from school activities or child care, use this time to unwind together and learn about each other's day.

- Take a daily walk. Spend twenty minutes outside together. This is a great way to inspire conversation, get some physical activity and avoid in-home distractions.

Work on implementing strategies that can help you better manage your household. Remember, don't try to do too many things at once or you will just overwhelm yourself. Choose a place to start, and then continue to implement more management-tactics as time goes on.

RESOURCES FOR MANAGING THE SINGLE-PARENT HOUSEHOLD

Simple Pleasures Press offers practical and encouraging help for people looking for ways to simplify their lives. Help includes money saving ideas, frugal living, simple cooking and more. Send a SASE for a brochure describing the *Simple Living* booklet and/or the *Frozen Assets* book. A free brochure filled with money saving ideas for the holidays is also available for a SASE. Send your request to: Simple Pleasures Press, Post Office Box 941, Auburn, WA, 98071-0941. Or visit their web site at: *http://members.aol.com/Dsimple/index.htm* and *http://members.aol.com/OAMCLoop/index.html*

HOLIDAYS

Family Traditions: Celebrations for Holidays and Everyday by Elizabeth Berg, published by Readers Digest. Hundreds of activities, ideas, rituals and special celebrations are offered to enhance the family.

ORGANIZATION

The Get Organized! News helps individuals get control of their lives by offering organizational tips for daily activities in order to make more time for fun activities. Subscription price is $14 a year for 12 issues. Visit their web site for tips and information at: *http://www.tgon.com*

Five Days To An Organized Life, by Lucy Hedrick. Published by Dell Publishing. Request this book from your local bookstore or call (800) ALL-BOOK to order. $8.95. This easy and practical guide follows a five step program to create organization, manage time and help readers reach both professional and personal goals.

QUICK AND EASY MEAL PREPARATION

Several books are available on the subject and the Internet offers a wealth of information. Here are some sources to get you started:

BOOKS FOR ADVANCE COOKING AND PREPARATION

Frozen Assets by Deborah Taylor-Hough. Published by Simple Pleasures Press. "Whether you call it once-a-month cooking, cooking ahead or bulk cooking, the concept is still the same—creating a stock of homemade meals in your freezer. This simple, common sense method of cooking and menu planning saves time, effort and money. You may choose to cook all day and stock up a month's worth or meals or you might spread your bulk cooking out over the course of several days. You may decide to cook freezer meals periodically, taking advantage of sales on meat. You might like to double or triple recipes as you cook during the week, adding the extra batches to your stash of *Frozen Assets*. Whatever method of cooking for the freezer you choose, you'll find *Frozen Assets* to be a wise, money-saving, time-saving investment in your family's health and well-being." For ordering information for the book, *Frozen Assets*, or for a free brochure, write to: *Simple Pleasures Press, PO Box 941, Auburn, WA 98071-0941.*

Once-A-Month Cooking by Mimi Wilson and Mary Beth Lagerborg. Published by Focus on the Family, 1994.

Dinners in the Freezer: More Mary and Less Martha by Jill Bond. Published by G C B Pub Group, April 1996.

Cook Now Serve Later by Readers Digest. Published by Readers Digest, May 1990.

WEB SITES FOR ADVANCE COOKING AND PREPARATION

Cooking for a Day / Eat for a Month - This is a great introductory web site to this cooking method.
http://members.aol.com/oamcloop/index.html

The On-Line Cookbook by Dawn Wise is another valuable resource complete with shopping lists. Visit the site at
http://www.wisepub.com/cookpg1.htm

Busy Cooks offers links to many valuable sites.
http://busycooks.miningco.com/msubrecipes.htm

CHAPTER FOUR

BALANCING WORK AND FAMILY

Among our survey participants, many single parents reported feeling guilty for thinking about work when spending time with their children or feeling guilty when thinking of family while working. Inside this Catch-22, parents reported feeling that neither their work nor their family was receiving undivided attention. It is possible to find a median to balance these two important roles.

By implementing a few basic strategies, single parents can turn their home into a team environment where a family works together. Let's get started with some work basics and ways you can successfully balance the roles of employee (or employer) and parent.

Some single parents try to keep work and family completely separate. While this a good goal, it isn't always possible. It's good to take some basic steps for combining work and family for the benefit of both you and your children. Here are a few ideas to try:

Explain your work. Young children may not comprehend the dynamics of work. It is good to sit down and explain that working is how one affords the day-to-day needs of food, etc. There is no need to go into explicit explanations when an overview will do.

Let children into your world. Try to share a funny story or two from work during dinner. This will help ease young children's curiosities or worries about where you are during the day. For teens, it helps them to see how you act in a role outside of mom or dad.

Take Pictures. Take your child's pictures or artwork to your place of employment. (If there are no places to display the items, carry a small picture or photo book with you.) Let your child know that you are taking the artwork and showing it to co-workers. Pass on any compliments co-workers give your child. It's a good idea to also let your child see your place of employment and to see the pictures and art projects that you proudly display.

Have a plan. Days will undoubtedly come where you will be unable to attend a child's school event or a child will be ill. Make sure to discuss these circumstances with your boss and to ask for a bit of leeway should your child be sick or should you need to pick him up from school.

Some single parents have very understanding work environments, while others find they can get no leniency from their schedule. If you are of the latter group, devise a back up plan. Contact a local child care agency for back-up ideas or ask a relative or friend to be your back-up. Extracurricular activities may also create occasional conflicts. If you have to miss a special event, offer an alternative support person. A close older friend, relative or Big Brother, Big Sister program can offer someone to attend the event and support your child. Catch up when you can, and then offer to take all attendees out for dinner or host a cookout. Get the full scoop and all the details of the event from your child. This allows your child to relive the excitement of the event.

> Realize that no matter how hard you try, there will be times when no one gets along. Grab a friend and talk or cry or eat. A couple of hours later, you will be ready to deal with things again.
>
> *Rhonda Sayre*
> *Billings, Montana*

Find support at work. Try to make friends with other single parents that you can share frustrations and triumphs with. This can be great for day-to-day support, an occasional lunch—or even helping each other in an emergency situation. Make sure this doesn't turn into a "dump" session where you speak negatively about ex-partners, problems, etc. It's fine to discuss these things briefly but try to then come to a resolution on the issue.

Lunch hours. If you find yourself short on time with your children, consider using an occasional lunch hour to catch up. Choosing a day care facility that is close to work can allow you to do this while also making pick up and drop off easier.

Have a happy hour with your kids. Once everyone arrives home have some sparkling cider in fancy glasses and a happy hour. Take 30 minutes or an hour to catch up on current events in each other's lives.

Have a designated "turn off" point. When you leave work focus on unwinding. If you have a short commute, drive a longer route. Turn on some nice music and work on clearing your head from the day's responsibilities and focusing on unwinding for family time.

Don't take work home.* Avoid taking work home whenever possible. Even if you plan on not working until after the kids are in bed, it creates a distraction and will only add to the pressure of having too much to do. Instead, try to delegate work out or start a little earlier. If you must bring work home from time to time, leave your briefcase in the trunk of your car until after your kids have gone to bed. Work on keeping your time "at home" mostly for the kids.

***What if you work at home?** For those of us who work at home we can't very well keep our work out of the house. Our goal is to keep our work out of our family life. I have always found it challenging to close the door on work with it being so nearby. But to avoid burnout and to devote time to our families, it's important to keep a structured work week that allows time for yourself and for your family.

Some of us face the additional challenge of working at home while our young children are present. There can be a great tug of emotions between devoting time to your child or your work. If part-time or full-time outside care is not an option, devise a structured work week that allows for time with your child periodically throughout the day while also allowing time for your work.

THE MORNING CRUNCH

Do your mornings feel more like a push and pull contest rather than a smooth preparation for the day ahead? Finding items that need to be taken to school, feeding pets, walking dogs, last minute planning on who will be home when, getting everyone dressed, coping with the child who'd rather be sleeping, making breakfast—these are just a few of the commonly reported challenges facing single parents every morning.

There are tips and tricks to alleviate the morning crunch. Try the following for a smoother morning routine.

- The thirty-minute prep. If morning feels more like a race track than a time of controlled preparation, practice the 30-minute prep. Ease morning responsibilities by preparing all you can the night before. Have children set their clothes out, put toys away and pack their school bags before bed. Set your own clothes out. After dinner, routinely set the breakfast table complete with cereal boxes, bowls and silverware. Set up your coffee maker so you can simply press the "on" button in the morning. Bag lunches. Whatever you can do in thirty minutes at night will be thirty minutes less awaiting you in the morning when people aren't running at their best.

- Keep it simple. While television may glamorize a gorgeous family sitting down to pancakes made in the shape of hearts, the practical parent knows the value of simplicity—cereal or toast. Save time-consuming breakfasts for a weekend treat or assign one night a week as "breakfast for dinner" night.

- Listen to the weather ahead of time to guide children in clothing choices.

- Have children lay out their clothes and pack their own lunches. This can be a good responsibility for a chore and reward system.

- Place your clothes out the night before. Place your keys, briefcase, etc. near the door.

- Give "warnings" that the bus is leaving 30 minutes, 15 minutes and five minutes prior to departure to keep kids on track.

- Make sure kids have clocks in their bedrooms to monitor time.

- Take it one thing at a time. Instead of wrestling with getting both yourself and your children ready in the morning, get up an hour early so that you are dressed and showered before your children arise.

- Encourage children's promptness with a mark on their reward chart or, if you give allowance, let morning preparation be one of the responsibilities that helps children earn it.

- If you have only one bathroom, prepare a bathroom schedule and let kids be responsible for getting in and out on time.

DESIGNING RELAXING EVENINGS

After a long day's work many parents look forward to a relaxing evening at home. Yet a parent arrives home only to be bombarded with news broadcasts of their child's events, demands for dinner, housework that needs to be done, homework that needs to be assisted with, baths and teeth to be brushed, laundry to be done, next day events to be organized—the beat goes on.

> Enjoy simple things with your children and change the routines to fit your lifestyle. Try eating Kid Cuisine one night a week or having a simple cheese, cracker and fruit dinner on the rug.
> *Sue Hendricks*
> *Gainesville, Florida*

Evenings can be the enjoyable time you would like for both your children and yourself. Preplanning and sticking to a regular schedule will maximize your time together.

Look at the time you have in the evening and break it up into increments to cover your evening goals. Here is how one single parent's schedule looks:

5:30-6:00	Pick up kids from Susan's and drive home.
6:00-6:30	We all sit in the kitchen for "Happy Hour" and talk while one of us prepares dinner.
6:30 - 9:00	A nice sit down dinner. Afterwards I load the dishes and kids start their homework from 7:30-9. While kids work on their homework I catch up on bill-paying, phone calls, permission slips, etc. If they finish early, we play a card game together.
9:00-9:30	Kids prepare for the next day while I veg on the couch.
9:30	Lights out for kids and I curl up with a book.

As you plan your evening schedule, allot time for the following:

- Your own relaxation
- Time together as a family
- A sit-down dinner when possible. (Note: this doesn't mean a full course meal with a representative from all food groups. It simply means everyone's bottom on a chair while chewing through whatever the menu is. Whether it be TV dinners, macaroni or cereal is irrelevant.)
- One-on-one time with each child (alternate nights if necessary)
- Homework
- Next day preparations

KEYS FOR CREATING RELAXING EVENINGS

- When you arrive home from work, take a minute to switch gears and change into something more comfortable.

- If homework hassles are giving you a headache, create a work hour. Perhaps after dinner, but before dessert, have one hour devoted to homework. While children work on their homework, take time to catch up on your own reading or paperwork.

- Murphy's Law should state "the more you try to relax the more you will think of that which needs to be done." Make a habit of keeping to-do lists in your car, at work and at home. If you think of something that needs to be done, jot it down so it isn't weighing on your mind.

* Get moving! Work off the day's stresses and spend some quality time with the kids by moving. Enjoy a physical activity together (outside if possible) like basketball, kickball or climbing a tree. Just 20 minutes outside after a long day can help parents and kids unwind, de-stress and catch up. If the weather won't permit a trip outside, try a quick game of charades (each family member takes one turn) or turn on some music and dance.

* Avoid the phone. Let the answering machine pick up the calls at night while you are spending time with your children.

* Make a list with your child of ten things you would really like to do together. Aim to do one every other week.

BUSINESS TRIPS

If your work requires regular travel, special home preparations will need to be made. Remember the following:

A Medical Authorization. If you leave your child in the care of another relative or a sitter, make sure to leave an emergency medical authorization like the one in the resource section of this chapter.

Numbers, Comforts, Allergies and More. A three-ring-binder works best for storing information since you can add and change the pages easily. In your binder, be as thorough as you like. Items to definitely include are:

* List of allergies
* List of immunizations
* Doctor contact for day and night hours
* Emergency contact numbers
* Poison Control
* Local friends and family who can be contacted
* School phone numbers
* A copy of your itinerary, flight numbers, hotels, etc.

- Medical Authorization (a sample form is included in the resources section of this chapter)

Other items you might want to include:

- List of your child's "routine"
- What your child really enjoys
- Favorite Foods / Foods Disliked
- CPR Instructions
- First Aid Instructions

JOB BURNOUT

If your job is wearing you down, don't give up. You can change your life. If you have a marketable job skill, research options and alternative careers. The amount of time we spend working each week is too large a commitment to spend it in a way that leaves us unsatisfied.

If you are in a dead-end job, or lack a marketable job skill, there is much that you can do to change this. See the resources section of this chapter for ideas to get you started down this path.

> Do not try to be super mom or super dad, just be yourself and the children will accept you for who you are.
> *Earl Husser*
> *Bossier City, Louisiana*

The first step in dealing with job dissatisfaction is determining what precisely is leaving you frustrated. Is it the actual work that you are performing? Is it the structural environment? Is it a co-worker or boss? Is it the hours and the demands? Once you have pinpointed what is causing your frustration, you will have a better handle on how to remedy it.

WHY ARE YOU DOING SO MUCH?

If you find that week after week you are inundated with workloads that never seem to let up, ask yourself, "Why am I doing so much?" Mental health professionals agree that many people overwork in order to avoid other issues in their life that may be bothersome. If you feel this might describe you, speak with a counselor or use other educational materials to look into the symptoms of a workaholic. If this doesn't describe you, consider the following options to relieve the stresses of work:

Flex Time. Flex time is a popular variation of the full-time work week. Instead of putting in a 9 to 5 day, employees can choose their own 40 hours, as long as it still fits the company's needs. If Flex time sounds of interest to you, talk to your human resources department to see if anyone is currently doing it. If no one is, make a proposal for your boss and think through objections beforehand.

Telecommuting. Telecommuting allows workers to do a portion of their work at home, thus saving commuting time. Companies haven't hopped on this bandwagon too quickly, since most employers still like to oversee their employees.

Part Time Work. Review the financial section of this book carefully. There could be ways to minimize your finances and work a few less hours per week. Even 35 hours compared to 40 can make a world of difference. If you know that money is too strapped to consider this option now, work through the financial section and make it a goal.

If your current job is the problem and not the structure of the job, keep your eyes and ears open for other opportunities. Ideas for job searches are included in the resources section of this chapter.

> Don't be hard on yourself. You can't be doctor, nurse, mom, dad, teacher, cook, cleaner, etc., all at one time.
> *S. Tackmann*
> *Lake City, Minnesota*

Balancing work and family is one of the hardest responsibilities to learn to juggle. With time and patience you can master the art of this delicate balance.

RESOURCES FOR BALANCING WORK AND FAMILY

The following pamphlets are available free or for a minimal charge from the Consumer Information Center. Request them by document number and title from The Consumer Information Center, Pueblo, CO 81009. If a fee is required, please include a check with your order. Or visit their web site at *http://www.pueblo.gsa.gov/*

High Earning Workers Who Don't Have a Bachelor's Degree - This 8 page brochure lists more than 100 occupations requiring less than a college degree. Send $1.00 along with your request for pamphlet 101D.

OSHA: Employee Workplace Rights - This 19 page brochure lets you know what to do if you question the safety of, or hazards in, your workplace. Includes contacts for additional help and information. Pamphlet 617D is free.

Resumes, Application Forms, Cover Letters and Interviews - This 8 page brochure offers tips for tailoring your resume for specific jobs and sample interview questions. Send $1.00 with your request for pamphlet 102D.

Tips for Finding the Right Job. Learn how to assess your skills and interests, prepare a resume, write cover letters and interview for a job. This 28 page pamphlet is available for $1.75, ask for brochure 131D.

Telecommute America describes the kinds of jobs appropriate for work at home or in satellite offices. Lists the benefits, requirements and skills needed, and how to present work at home ideas to management. This 12 page brochure is free. Request item 590C.

Occupational Outlook Quarterly reviews new occupations, salaries, job trends and more. A one-year subscription (4 issues) is $9.50. Ask for 250D.

Tomorrow's Jobs discusses changes in the economy, labor force, future demand and more. This 14 page brochure is available for $1.75. Item 103D.

What You Should Know About Your Pension Rights explains your rights, benefits, payment schedules, protections and more. Send .50 cents for this 48 page brochure. Item 359D.

The Job Outlook in Brief: 1992-2005. For $3.00 this 48 page brochure projects job prospects for nearly 250 occupations to the year 2005. Details anticipated demand, deadline, related jobs and more. Item 105C.

Matching Yourself With the World of Work. Requirements, prospects and earnings are listed for 200 occupations. 13 pages, $1.00. Item 106C.

WOMEN

Work & Family Clearing House, Women's Bureau (800) 827-5335

9 to 5 National Association of Working Women, 238 W. Wisconsin Ave., #900, Milwaukee, WI 53203. (800) 522-0925. Membership is $25 annually for an individual, $40 annually for an organization. Write or call to receive a copy of "Tips on Balancing Work and Family" excerpted from the book *9 to 5 Guide to Balancing Job/Family Challenge.*

When away from home, leave a medical authorization, like the one on the following page, with your child's caregiver.

SAMPLE MEDICAL AUTHORIZATION

I the undersigned parent of _____, a minor, author-ize _____ as agent(s) for all medical decisions regarding the minor's health and care. This includes, but is not limited to, anesthetics, medical and/or surgical diagnosis', X-ray examinations, and any needed or advised hospital care administered under any licensed* physician or surgeon.

This authorization is given to provide authority to the said agent to give specific consent to any and all such diagnosis, treatment or hospital care. The above named agent may exercise his/her best judgment for all medical decisions of above named minor.

_____   _____

(Parent's Signature)   (Date)

_____

(Print Name)

*(Licensed under provisions of the Medical Practice Act)

CHAPTER FIVE
PART ONE

CREATING A
SOLID FINANCIAL PLAN

The word "money" is enough to make many of us cringe. Caught behind a seemingly never ending crunch of expenses, or paycheck to paycheck living, we feel a bit overwhelmed. As one of my good friends always says, "Brook, you can teach me to budget my money when I have some, okay?" After a few years of reciting this line, she realized it was a dilemma not unlike the chicken and the egg. She still didn't have any money to manage. In order to get money, she had to budget the little that she had.

Money can be manageable, and the management can be rewarding. The more you know, the more confident you'll be in handling your investments and financial decisions. Throughout this chapter we'll dive into the issues that single parents mentioned as pertinent to their financial footing.

You may want to have a pen, paper and calculator handy. This chapter requires you to do some work, work that will literally pay off.

Before we get started, take stock of your current financial situation by answering the questions on the following page.

TAKING STOCK OF WHERE YOU ARE

	YES	NO
Do you have a monthly budget in place?	____	____
Do you have a current will drawn up?	____	____
Do you have a life insurance policy?	____	____
Have you anticipated college costs for your children and made any preparations or potential plans?	____	____
Do you have an emergency savings fund established?	____	____
Do you prepare your taxes on time and with ease?	____	____
Is your checkbook balanced regularly?	____	____
Have you begun saving for retirement either through work or on your own?	____	____
Do your family members have adequate health insurance coverage?	____	____
Do you know where your credit rating stands?	____	____
Have you investigated saving options besides a standard account to maximize your money's potential growth?	____	____
Do your children understand the value and concept of money?	____	____
Do you have adequate home (or renters) and auto insurance coverage?	____	____

How did you fair with your financial footing? Did you find you answered yes or no to most questions? Of the questions you answered "no," were there any that you wished you could have marked "yes?"

On the bottom of a sheet of paper, list your financial goals. Use the items that you wished you had marked "yes" as a springboard. Next to each goal, include a goal date by which you hope to accomplish this item.

You now know where you are and have an idea of where you'd like to be. It's time to figure out how to get there.

THE KEY TO SUCCESS

There is no way around it; a budget is required to take you from point A to point B. Just like in business, when plans are made, companies work within the resources available, to move from one goal to another. As you work to maximize your household financial position, a budget will be the most important key.

To design a budget system, you'll need a folder with several pockets to organize all your forms and receipts. Forget the fancy budget books, the worksheets and forms. I've tried enough of them to know that typically the expenses and layout aren't customizable for most families. It becomes more work than necessary. Instead, set out to make your own forms that are as basic as possible. This will give you a better chance at maintaining your budget system.

DESIGNING THE MONTHLY WORKSHEET

Perhaps the easiest way to make a monthly worksheet is to divide your expenses into two categories, fixed expenses and variable expenses. List out fixed expenses (those which do not vary). These might include: rent or mortgage, car payment, insurance, utilities, etc.

Under the variable expenses heading, list those items which either vary month to month or could be adjusted. These might include dry cleaning, groceries, phone bill, spending money, etc.

On the bottom of the page list your monthly income and then total each section, as illustrated in the sample.

SAMPLE MONTHLY WORKSHEET

Fixed Expenses	Amount	Variable Expenses	Amount
Rent	600	Phone	125
Insurance	50	Groceries	250
Car Payment	198	Entertainment	250
Electric	55		

Child Care	525		
Visa	100		
Income	2200 monthly		
Total Expenses	2,153		
Difference	47.00 for savings		

TAKING A REALISTIC LOOK
AT WHAT YOUR BUDGET REVEALS

Once you have your budget in writing, take a moment to analyze what it reveals about your financial situation.

If your income exceeds your expenses, is that money going into savings each month? If not, where is it going?

Does your budget include life insurance, health insurance, anticipated college costs?

Are there any categories that are receiving too much? Could you reduce any of the variable expenses without reducing the result? Instead of taking three children to a matinee, could a picnic be an ample and less expensive substitute?

Compare what your budget reveals against the goals you wrote down earlier. Can you identify some of the basic steps to help you move toward these goals?

HOW TO MAXIMIZE YOUR BUDGET

To optimize the effectiveness of your budget, track your expenses each month to make sure you are staying within the guidelines you have established.

As you get used to living within the guidelines of your budget, stay attentive for new options to save even more. Each month, try to implement one or two new strategies for saving an extra five to ten dollars.

Analyze your progress each month to make sure the budget is growing with your household. Re-figure as necessary.

ITEMS ON THE BUDGET

The more specific the budget the better. The example budget is broad in scope so that it's easy to use. Set up your budget to be as specific as you are comfortable with. The more detailed the budget, the more you will be able to track your dollars and deduce extra opportunities for stashing savings.

Choose from the following items as you establish your budget. Add others as they occur to you.

HOUSING

Mortgage or rent	Gas	Water & Sewer
Electric	Property taxes	House Insurance
Phone	Yard maintenance	Improvements
Cleaning help	Home equity loans	

FOOD

Groceries	Restaurant	Work lunches

CLOTHING

You	Children

TRANSPORTATION

Car payments	Auto insurance/ Auto repair
Bus Fares, Cab Fares, etc.	Gas
Maintenance	

ENTERTAINMENT

Kids activities & hobbies	Family activities
Adult activities	Club memberships
Subscriptions	Vacations

MISCELLANEOUS

Gifts for children	Gifts for others	Investments
Unexpected Expenses		

CREDIT CARDS & LOANS

Mastercard/Visa/etc.   Student Loans

Personal Loans

CHILD CARE

Daycare   Baby-sitters   Camps

Extracurricular Activities

EDUCATION

Fees for children   College savings

Fees for advancing your personal interests

HEALTH CARE

Prescriptions   Health insurance   Dental

Eye Care

OTHER INSURANCE

Life   Disability

INCOME

Work income   Self-Employment   Alimony

Child Support   Social Security

Investment Income

FOR THOSE WHO REFUSE TO BUDGET

Think of your finances in terms of life's energy. This is not as new age as it sounds. This is a very simple tactic that can help you put both life and finances into perspective. The idea comes from Vicki Robin, bestselling author of *Your Money or Your Life*.

Take a piece of paper and jot down your yearly income. Next, subtract the cost of working from your yearly income. (The cost of working would include gas, car maintenance, lunches, child care, dry cleaning, special clothes—any expenses you incur by working.) Once you have subtracted these expenses you have your annual net income. Divide this number by the total hours you work in a year.

Here is an example of how this works. Julie makes $26,000 a year gross. After taxes and her IRA she has roughly $18,000 left. She has one two-year-old daughter who is in day care. Her day care expense is $140.00 per week for a total of $7280.00 a year. She commutes fifteen miles to work. That's a total of 30 miles a day. She multiplies 30 miles by the government rate of .315 cents a mile, times the number of days she works. That totals $2340.00 annually. Julie says she eats lunch out about twice a week, with her average meal costing $7.00. She also gets one or two sodas (.75 each) during the day and grabs a cup of coffee on the way to work. That's .80 cents. Add those items together for an annual total of $1170.00. Her dry-cleaning bills are about $40.00 a month and she spends another $40.00 on clothes, pantyhose, etc. for a total of $960 annually.

If we take all these totals from Julie's net income we see she is working for about $6250.00 per year. Divide that by the 2000 hours she works and she is netting $3.12 per hour.

What good is knowing this number? This is the best way to spend less without budgeting.

According to Robin you need to ask yourself, "Is this item worth this much of my life energy?" The next time you are looking at a $30.00 shirt, ask yourself, "Is this shirt worth ten hours (or six hours, or fourteen hours) of my time?" If it is, buy it. If it isn't, don't. Ask yourself this of everything—food, dinner out, etc.

FINANCIALLY OVER YOUR HEAD

So far we've analyzed where unaccounted money might disappear to. But what if the shoe is on the other foot, and the expense column looms higher than your income?

Unfortunately, many families can relate all too well to this dilemma. With the cost of child-raising escalating and the income and standard of living of many single-parent headed households decreasing after a divorce, these money pits are all too familiar.

ARE YOU MAXIMIZING YOUR CURRENT SKILLS?

After you apply the previous techniques for working with your budget, your work situation is the next area to check.

Are you being paid what you're worth? Spend an afternoon at the library and research your profession and those that are similar. What is the salary range, and are you at the high or low end of that range? Look in the paper and research what other companies are paying. If you find you aren't being adequately compensated, make plans to speak with your employer about a raise or increased benefits. If you have tried this already, consider submitting resumes to companies that you know compensate their employees closer to their worth.

Is overtime an option? If your budget woes are temporary and you feel money will only be tight for a month or two—consider overtime as a possibility for regaining your financial footing.

EXTRA MONEY, INDEPENDENCE AND REWARDS

Many people are doing it. Many people dream of doing it. Many people have the dream of owning their own successful home-based business.

And now more than ever that dream is being recognized by people throughout the country. With evolving technology, more and more people have access to the equipment needed for running home-based businesses. Corporate downsizing has also become a trend, creating a need for subcontractors.

The job market has become less secure. According to Barbara Brabec, author of *Homemade Money*, the rate of announced layoffs in midsummer 1991 was 2,500 people a day (in the United States). During the last 16 months of the 1991-92 recession, Fortune 500 companies released more than 600,000 people through early retirement plans or layoffs.

With this downsizing movement, more and more people are realizing the security offered by a home-run business. After all, you would not fire yourself, would you?

There are many options for working at home. Few people have the resources needed to leave their full-time gigs to start a home-based business, however most owners begin by "moonlighting." They develop their business plan and idea and then test it for its plausibility while still secure in their "day job" with a full-time income. If the idea proves plausible, they can then determine what income level they must reach in order to make a smooth transition from their full-time job. Then it's just a process of devising a goal and timeline to follow.

HOW MANY HATS CAN YOU WEAR?

If you thought you were busy enough now, be ready to add a few more hats to your wardrobe. Odds are when you begin your business you will be the president, the accountant, the marketing director and the customer support department. Your first months or years will be far from glamorous. Take a realistic look at your time and commitments. How much time do you have to devote to your business? Businesses can be started within the smallest allowances of time. Just realize that the business will grow in proportion to the time devoted to its development.

RESEARCH, RESEARCH, RESEARCH

The next step is research. Begin by talking to anyone who is in the type of business you hope to enter. Call them. Offer to take them to lunch. Most people love to share their knowledge. They feel honored and you can get some inside tips and avoid the timely mistakes they made when starting out.

Visit the library and gather any books to help you research your business idea. You may need to research suppliers, learn sales techniques, or learn how to do your own bookkeeping. Take an afternoon to stock up on some reading.

On the way home from the library stop at your courthouse or city office. Find out if you need any licenses to run your business in your home. Check on zoning and regulations.

SERVICE OR PRODUCT?

There are two basic types of businesses: product-oriented and service-oriented. Product-oriented businesses sell a product such as cosmetics, computers or office supplies. Service-oriented businesses provide a service such as tax preparation, child care, housecleaning or billing services.

The first step in choosing your home-based business is to ask which category your talents and your preferences fall into. Do you have a specific skill that you could market as a service? Or do you find that selling products is more to your liking? Remember that in service-oriented businesses you will often be dealing with people more than in product-oriented business. Take a look back at your past jobs. Were they product or service-oriented? Which were you drawn to, and which did you enjoy most?

CAPITAL

One of your next considerations in choosing a home-based business will be how much money you need. If you already own a computer and have an accounting degree, doing accounting work would be a natural tie-in, requiring little capital to get started.

Take a pen and paper and write down any resources you have for generating capital. Check with your local Small Business Administration office for information on loans and grants.

GO IT ALONE OR NOT

Many entrepreneurs start from scratch. They form a business idea and then take the needed steps to bring it to fruition. But that isn't the only way to form a home-based business. There are many companies who have already ironed out the kinks. If time keeps you from starting from scratch or you know you don't want to deal with marketing or designing promotional material, you might want to consider a pre-existing business. Cosmetic and gift companies are just a few of the many that offer Independent Consultant titles to men and women seeking a home-based business. If you consider one of these businesses, make sure to read all the fine print and talk to as many people as you can who are involved with (or have been) the company as well as the Better Business Bureau.

IDEAS TO THINK ABOUT

The options for a home-based business are as varied as your imagination. Most people have a tendency to lean towards either providing a product or a service. Once you determine which is more rewarding for you, brainstorm a list of talents and interests to develop possible options for pursuing additional income. Here are a few ideas to get started:

Accounting	Direct Sales	Furniture Restoration
Desktop Publishing	Artist	Bookkeeper
Repair	Graphic Design	Photography
Tax Preparation	Cake Decorating	Child Care
Catering	Housecleaning	Billing Services

ITEMIZING EXPENSES

Begin jotting down all expenses that come to mind. Next, jot down an estimated monthly dollar amount for each expense. Total your expenses and add an extra 20%. This extra 20% provides a safety net and will cover unexpected expenses you might incur. Based on these rough figures, how much capital is needed to get stocked and started? How much will you need to maintain the first six months of operation?

Most businesses that fail, do so because of lack of capital or financial savvy. Make sure you have the financial means to back up the time you will be investing. If you are short on capital you have several options. Loans and grants from the SBA are one. Bank loans or credit lines are another source of funding. If these options are not available to you, do you know people who would be willing to invest? Is there someone you would be interested in forming a partnership with?

MARKETING PLAN

Next, you need to devise your marketing plan. By now you may have more than one idea for a business. A marketing plan and financial test can help you determine which idea is best.

How to let the world know that your business exists is the focus of the marketing plan. A spiral notebook is essential as you begin brainstorming all the ways to let future clients know of your new business. Continue adding to this notebook (and interview others for ideas) until you feel you have a solid foundation for launching your business. Then transfer your notes to a calendar and assign each marketing task to an actual date and dollar amount.

MAKE YOUR TIMELINE

Now that you have your marketing strategy and financial plan, you are ready to make a timeline. Purchase a monthly calendar and write in each project you must complete before launching your new endeavor. Be careful not to pack too much too closely. Allow yourself some extra time for those unexpected responsibilities that are bound to occur.

IF YOU ARE STILL IN CASH AND CREDIT CRISIS

If you find that after researching all possibilities you are still in a financial crisis that you cannot get out of, take immediate action to regain control of your financial future.

IMMEDIATE ACTION

- Log all your bills and their due dates in a section of your budget notebook. Send only the minimum payments and make sure to send at least something on each bill.

- Pay bills at the end of your grace period.

- Brainstorm any additional ways to gather funds. Do you have a relative or trusted friend that can help you through a trying time? Asking for help is better than damaging your credit.

- Are there any items that you can sell that do not hold great personal value?

- Consider seeking the aid of a debt counseling agency to help you create a repayment plan to your creditors and prepare a plan to avoid a cash crisis in the future. The resource section of this chapter lists several debt counseling services and informational brochures.

KNOW YOUR RIGHTS

If bill collectors are adding unneeded stress to your life, assert your legal rights. Emily Card and Christine Watts Kelly report the following in their book, *The Single Parent's Money Guide*, *"Collectors have no right to call you early in the morning or late at night. They have no right to call you at work once you have asked them not to in writing. For that matter, once you ask not be called in writing creditors cannot call you unless they intend to take more formal legal steps.*

"Creditors and collection agencies all too often violate these procedures, so log any calls you receive including the time and date, and use this evidence against the collector. Many a consumer debt has been forgiven in exchange for consumers' not suing overly aggressive collectors.

> The authors of *The Single Parent's Money Guide* have a web-site online. Visit it for valuable tips and information on how to order their informative book.
>
> *http://www.womenmoney.com*

Also, get an answering machine and use it to filter unwanted calls. You have no obligation to talk to hordes of angry collectors, thereby making your mental outlook more difficult."

BANKRUPTCY: THE RUMORS, THE REALITY

Sometimes bankruptcy will be the only key to starting fresh. Be fore-warned—the implications may impact your credit for up to ten years. If possible, try to seek an alternative method before taking this more permanent measure.

If bankruptcy is your only option, speak to an attorney for help in which code is best for your situation. Contact your local division of the State Bar Association for a bankruptcy lawyer referral.

ESTABLISHING CREDIT

In the transition to a single-parent home, many custodial parents find that they have little of their own credit since much of it was shared jointly with a spouse. If you do not have a credit history, you should begin to build one.

The Federal Trade Commission offers the following tips for obtaining credit:

If you have a steady income and have lived in the same area for at least a year, try applying for credit with a local business such as a department store. Or you might borrow a small amount from your credit union or the bank where you have checking and savings accounts. A local bank or department store may approve your credit application even if you don't meet the standards of larger creditors. Before you apply for credit, ask whether the creditor reports credit history information to credit bureaus serving your area. Most creditors do, but some do not. If possible, you should try to get credit that will be reported. This builds your credit history.

If you are rejected for credit, find out why. There may be reasons other than lack of credit history. Your income may not meet the creditor's minimum requirement, or you may not have worked at your current job long enough. Time may resolve such problems. You could wait for a salary increase and then reapply, or simply apply to a different creditor. However, it is best to wait at least six months before making each new application. Credit bureaus record each inquiry about you. Some creditors may deny your application if they think you are trying to open too many new accounts too quickly.

HOW TO IMPROVE YOUR CREDIT

If inaccurate information plagues your credit report, you are entitled by law to correct it. When an application for credit is rejected, the creditor must identify the credit bureau from which it obtained information. At this point, contact the credit bureau for disclosure of the contents of your credit file. If this request is made within thirty days of being turned down, there is no charge for the credit information.

Once you have your credit file, check to make sure the report is accurate and complete. If you find an error, you have the right, under the Fair Credit Reporting Act, to dispute the information. Notify the credit bureau in writing of why you feel the report is in error and keep a copy for your records.

The credit bureau must investigate all matters which are relevant to your credit status. The Federal Trade Commission tells us that "the credit bureau must correct any information that it finds is not reported accurately. Information that cannot be verified must be deleted. If you disagree with the results of the credit bureau's reinvestigation, you may file a brief dispute statement explaining your side of the story. At your request, the credit bureau will note your dispute in future credit bureau reports. Be aware that when negative information in your report is accurate, only the passage of time can assure its removal. Credit bureaus are permitted by law to report bankruptcies for ten years and other negative information for seven years."

MONEY-SAVING TIPS

Have a plan (and then follow it) at the grocery store. It's obvious to have a list. In fact, I'm great at list-making. On my last dash to the store, my list contained the following items: Wheat Chex, toothpaste, gallon of milk, cheddar cheese, pretzels and Gatorade. The bill should have easily totaled less than $25.00. By the time I neared the checkout, my bill totaled close to $50.00. It seems a few extra items had crept into my cart. Make sure you have a plan and then *follow it* when you do your shopping. If you continually overspend (like I have the tendency to do) leave the house with what you plan to spend plus a $5.00 leeway.

Put kids to work clipping coupons. Single parents rarely have the time to clip coupons for savings. Give your children a list of products that you use regularly. Sit them down each Sunday with the paper and let them partake in a coupon hunt. For each coupon they find (and you use), they get to keep half of the coupon's value. For example; if they find a $1.00 off coupon on Cheerios, they receive .50 cents when you use it and your grocery bill bottom line receives the other .50 cents.

Watch where you walk. Less expensive items are typically placed around the outside of the market, it's those middle aisles that hold the items that quickly add to your bill. When you do need to dash down one of those aisles, remember to look high and look low. Less expensive items are usually placed near the top or bottom of the shelves. The shelves that are eye-level are reserved for the more expensive items.

Buy in bulk when you can. Buying items, that don't spoil, in bulk can save money and save trips to the store. For staples and nonperishable goods, stock up at good sale prices or join a warehouse club. If warehouse quantities are too much for your own family, combine your list with a few other single parents and then split the food to maximize your savings.

Let children design greeting cards and wrapping paper using items found around the house. This makes a great rainy day project while providing savings for the family.

WHAT'S FOR DINNER?

If the "what's for dinner" syndrome plagues your household and the next thing you know the Pizza Man is appearing at your door, use a menu planning system. Give each night a "theme" so the question of dinner-fixings doesn't linger. For example, let your children cook Saturday night. If Wednesdays tend to be hectic, plan on something easy like macaroni & cheese, spaghetti or pizza.

Shop year round. Instead of waiting for Christmas woes and stressing at a time that should be joyous for families, learn to shop and take advantage of sales year around. Have a small amount taken from each paycheck and put into a Christmas fund. Carry a Christmas list in your daily planner.

If you haven't tried a thrift shop, now is the time. While the idea of thrift and resale shops once brought to mind pictures of dingy rooms with stained clothes— not so anymore! Thrift shop business is booming. If you haven't tried a second-hand store, take a peek, you could be pleasantly surprised!

> ## QUICK CHECK
>
> How many times did you eat out or opt for drive through meals over the past week? Sit back and try to recall. Total up the amounts. Could that come out of your budget? Home-cooked meals encourage family time while also slashing expenses.

Keep a spending diary. If you find that you are still scrimping day to day, keep a detailed spending journal. It is often amazing how little purchases add up to big expenses! Seeing expenses in black and white can be eye opening. Buying a quick cup of coffee at a drive-through each morning can easily cost you $20-$30 a month. Most people spend at least $5.00 each weekday on food related items at work. (Lunch, pop, coffee, snacks, etc.) Bringing lunches, treats and drinks from home could save your family $100 per month—or $1200 per year! Little expenses add up quickly if they're done on a regular basis.

When you find the areas in your life where the money is draining out, plug up the holes! Now that you are better equipped to handle your current finances, let's take a look ahead to finances of the future.

CHAPTER FIVE
PART TWO
CREATING A SOLID
FINANCIAL PLAN
FOR THE FUTURE

With the hectic pace of the present, plans for the future can get set aside and before we know it, the future is here and we are unprepared. Make time to avoid this pitfall by laying a foundation and strategy for your savings and your future.

PLANNING AHEAD FOR COLLEGE DAYS

Stocks - When starting early enough, stocks offer a great option for college savings. When my daughter was born, I invested $1000 in a variety of stocks. By the time she reached 2½ this had already

The United States Department of Agriculture estimates that it costs $239,000 adjusted for inflation, to raise one child, not including college.

In 1995 the average annual cost for private college including books, room and board, and tuition was $11,522 for private and $2,869 for public schools.

grown to $4000. With the stock market, however, there is always a level of risk. Diversifying and learning about the market is key. Don't let the market intimidate you. I stopped in a local broker's office and confessed that I knew nothing. Within an hour he had provided me with a brief low-down, reading materials and my new account information.

Mutual Funds - If you're leery of the stock market or don't have ample time for research, check into mutual funds. These offer the benefits of professionals to manage your money, and you can make automatic payments into the fund, thus guaranteeing you will be saving. A mutual fund pools investors' money over a selection of stocks, bonds and other securities. This provides diversification versus the option of stock purchasing where you must diversify yourself. Different mutual funds have different requirements. Some require an initial investment of $1000 or more, while others offer an investment of $50 to $100 each month.

US Savings Bonds - While these won't provide the growth that the above two options offer, they do not have the risk either. The government-backed Series EE Savings Bonds are popular with parents. Available in increments of $50-$10,000 they offer several tax advantages. The income on these bonds is exempt from state and local tax. Federal tax is only paid when the bond is cashed in. For those families with incomes below $40,000, there may be no tax on earned interest if all the money is used for college and the bond was purchased by an adult after January 1, 1990. Be careful when cashing in bonds for college tuition—the revenue may be added to your income and could disqualify your child from some loans or grants.

Zero Coupon bonds - Like US Savings Bonds, Zero Coupon bonds are a good investment for those who want to know exactly what money will be put in and exactly what money the investor will get out. Purchasing a zero coupon bond locks you in at the current interest rate, a smart move if you believe interest rates are going to drop. If you think the interest rate may increase, a variable interest-rate bond is a better bet. Zero coupon bonds pay a lump sum at maturity rather than periodic interest like conventional bonds.

Home Equity - If you are leaning in the direction of a loan, a home equity loan can be a great option if you have enough equity built up in your home. Borrowing against your home offers a reduction of income tax since the interest is deductible. Compare rates against student loans to find your best value.

Keep in mind that virtually all investments other than those backed by the U.S. Government do have some level of risk. With most investments, a good rule of thumb is to never invest more than you can afford to lose.

LIFE INSURANCE

Providing for children, in the event something should happen to the custodial parent is a precaution that is important to take. All parents should have a will and life insurance (when affordable). The following guidelines can steer you in a direction for life insurance coverage.

Deciding on The Amount of Coverage.

To determine the coverage you will need, to provide ample care for your children, use the following formula:

1. Number of years income will need to be provided

    (typically until children reach an age to earn

    enough to support themselves)   _____

2. Estimated amount children will need each year   _____

Multiply Amount in Question 1 by Question 2.   _____

This provides an estimate of how much coverage will be needed.

Types of policies

Term - The most economical of coverage. You pay a yearly premium for a specific death benefit. The premium increases with age.

Whole - While more expensive than term, this policy builds a cash value and you may also borrow against it. Additionally, the premium is fixed for the full life of the policy, protecting the consumer against increases.

Universal Life - Is a newer form of insurance that allows more flexibility than the previous options. Your death benefit, cash value and length of premium payments can vary over the years. You can also raise or lower both the death benefit and the premiums throughout your life. These policies are, however, interest sensitive.

Variable Life - Another, newer policy where you can choose the investment options for your premium. While these do provide life insurance along with investment options their appropriateness depends on your financial circumstances.

Using this knowledge as a springboard, contact a local life insurance agent to see how the different types of policies can benefit your family.

WHERE THERE'S A WILL, THERE'S YOUR WAY
by Barbara J. Walton

Barbara J. Walton is an attorney practicing family law in northwestern Pennsylvania. She obtained her law degree from the University of Miami in Coral Gables. Divorced twice, she is the mother of three, step-parent of four, all teenagers—except one.

A will is a legal document which lets those handling your affairs following your death know your wishes. Your wishes may change over time as you get married, have children, get divorced, or have various relationships. As your life status changes, your will should, too.

If you don't have a will, distribution of property will fall under a statutory system known as intestacy, which has a formulaic division in black and white. For example, it could be that the spouse is entitled to half, and the children are entitled to the second half in equal shares. Each state has a scheme for this distribution in the absence of specific directions.

But what if you have children with special needs that you want to have a greater share of your estate? Or a spouse or child that you purposely want to exclude? This cannot happen unless you have the proper instructions in your will.

When you're ready to prepare a will, you should make a list of what items you specifically want to leave certain people. If your daughter has always wanted her great-grandmother's china and you want her to have it, the will should say so. I don't know how often I have been writing wills for clients, and they will tell me, "Oh my children are so agreeable, they'll just handle who gets what." It's sad to say, but by the time the will gets read, usually someone has absconded with precious items, while they were just "helping clean up" at the parent's house. Be specific.

You will also choose someone to make sure your debts are paid and wishes carried out. This person is called an executor or executrix (depending if it's a man or a woman). This person will take the will and file a probate case in court, collect any bills you owe at the time of your death and arrange payment from your assets, and make sure the children are taken care of as you have directed. You should choose an alternate executor as well, in case your first choice is for some reason unavailable when he's called upon.

Next, you will want to choose a guardian for your minor children. If their other parent is available the court will likely assign custody to them automatically, unless you have prepared ahead of time. If there is some compelling reason why your children's mother or father should not have custody under any circumstances (past abuse, etc.,) lay that out in detail in your will or in a document to be attached to it. You can instruct your executor on the steps you'd want taken.

There can be a separate guardian of the purse of the children; this would mean that any insurance proceeds or other assets left in the will to the children could be left to someone who would manage it. If your sister, for example, is a wonderful mother, but she hasn't the money management sense of a rabbit, you might want to designate her as the guardian of your child's person, so your child would be raised by her, and then name some person more fiscally responsible to handle the money.

If there are many assets or investments, the proper document to handle the passing of these assets may be a trust or other legal arrangement which would be managed by a third party. There may be methods of holding assets which have more or less favorable tax treatment, which would be worth exploring. To examine all your options, you should discuss your decisions with an attorney well-versed in the laws of your state.

Many kits are now available to help people prepare their own will. Software kits, books and forms at office stores are available for the creation of a will. It is important to check the laws in your state when using these tools. Some states require wills to be notarized, other states require a specific number of witnesses—while these tools can be a convenient option, make sure the will measures up to state regulations.

The important thing is to make your decisions now and let them be known by means of a will. That way, you can be assured your wishes will be considered and carried out. Any time you have a change in your status, like remarriage, more children, etc., you should make sure your will is updated accordingly.

HEALTH INSURANCE

If you are currently uninsured, take immediate steps to get coverage. Check with organizations that you belong to and see if a group rate is available. Health insurance is costly, but the cost of treatment is worse. One trip to the emergency room can pinch your finances for years to come.

Check around to find the best rate. Look into groups that offer group-rate discounts and consider joining. Even if the coverage is a high deductible, get coverage for in-hospital stays.

RETIREMENT

It is currently estimated that you'll need about 70% of your pre-retirement income in order to afford retirement. That number is higher for low-wage earners who will need 90% or more. Planning early is the key to developing a successful retirement.

To begin planning your retirement you must first know where you stand financially. In addition to creating your monthly budget, check out the following sources for a more complete picture:

Social Security pays approximately 40% of pre-retirement earnings. Call the Social Security Administration at (800) 772-1213 for a free Personal Earnings and Benefit Estimate Statement (PEBES.)

Check to see what your employee benefits are if your employer offers a plan. Learn what benefits you may have coming from prior employment. For a free booklet on private pensions, call the U.S. Department of Labor at (202) 219-8776.

After you have designed your budget and deducted as much as you can for savings and retirement, it's time to decide where this money should go. Check out the information on stocks and mutual funds at the beginning of this chapter for investment ideas. Also consider the following:

Contribute to a tax-sheltered savings plan if offered by your employer. Programs such as the 401(k) offer deferral of taxes and compounding of interest that add greatly to accumulated money over time. Since this money is also deducted from each check, it is less money that you will pay taxes on.

If your employer does not have a retirement plan, suggest that one be started. For information on simplified employee pensions (available to certain employers) call the Internal Revenue Service at (800) 829-3676 and request Internal Revenue Service Publication 590.

IRA's - Individual Retirement Accounts accept up to a capped dollar amount each year and allow you to delay paying taxes on investment earnings until retirement age. Internal Revenue Service Publication

590 (available by calling 800-829-3676) also contains information on IRAs.

Early planning will help to alleviate saving obstacles down the road. Take some time to plan out clear objectives for your future and investigate the best strategies to help you achieve those objectives.

RESOURCES FOR TAKING STOCK OF YOUR FINANCES AND PLANNING AHEAD

BANKRUPTCY

Bankruptcy is a five page pamphlet available from the Consumer Information Center. It explains what bankruptcy is, lists the different types and what the difference means in the short and long term. Request brochure 580D from the Consumer Information Center, Pueblo, CO 81009.

COLLEGE PLANNING

Scudder offers a great *Tuition Planning Worksheet*. Visit their web site at *http://funds.scudder.com/* From their home page choose "Interactive Worksheets."

The following five brochures are available free from the Consumer Information Center, Pueblo CO 81009. Or visit their web site at *http://www.pueblo.gsa.gov/*

All About Direct Loans. A 33 page booklet covering four types of direct student education loans; how much you can borrow, how to apply, how you'll be paid, repayment and more. Request booklet 516D.

Direct Student Loan Consolidation could benefit you financially. Learn how to consolidate your federal loans into a single account and more. 16 pages. Request booklet 517D.

Planning for College. Strategies to help you plan for tuition and fees along with helpful charts for estimating future costs. 10 pages. Request booklet 507D.

Preparing Your Child For College: A Resource Book for Parents. Work sheets and checklists to help plan for college academically and financially. 57 pages. Request brochure 508D.

Paying For College. How to estimate college expenses and put together a financing plan, including savings, financial aid, loans, grants, work study, etc. 24 pages. Request booklet 518D.

CREDIT INFORMATION AND ASSISTANCE

Copies of your credit report can be obtained from the credit bureaus. Call them directly at: Equifax 800-685-1111, Trans Union 316-636-6100. California residents should also call TRW at 800-422-4879.

For help in dealing with debts you can contact the Consumer Credit Counseling Service (CCCS). This nonprofit organization has more than 850 offices and its counselors will try to help arrange a repayment plan suitable to both you and your creditors. They can also assist in setting up a realistic budget plan for future expenses. These services are offered at little or no charge to you. Check your white pages for the nearest CCCS office, or use a touch-tone phone and call 800-388-2227.

If you have other questions on credit, write the National Foundation for Consumer Credit, Inc., 8611 Second Avenue, Suite 100, Silver Spring, MD 20910

The Federal Trade Commission offers several free brochures: *Women and Credit Histories*, *Fair Credit Reporting* and *Best Sellers*, which lists a variety of publications on credit and other consumer topics. Contact: Public Reference, Federal Trade Commission, Washington, DC 20580

ASSISTANCE WITH DEBT MANAGEMENT

A free brochure titled *Managing Your Debts: How To Regain Financial Health* is available for a self-addressed-stamped envelope. Request this brochure from: Consumer Federation of America, PO Box 12099, Washington, DC 20005.

A brochure titled *Fair Debt Collection* describes what debt collectors may and may not do if you owe money, as well as how and where to complain if you are harassed or threatened. This two page brochure is available for .50 cents from the Consumer Information Center, Pueblo, CO 81009.

FOR MORE INFORMATION
ON HOME-BASED BUSINESSES

Demographic and economic statistics for marketing purposes are available from the *Bureau of the Census*, Customer Services, Data User Services Division, Washington, DC 20233

For tax information, contact your local Internal Revenue Service. Some publications they can provide include: *Your Business Tax Kit; Business Use of Your Home; Determining Whether a Worker Is An Employee.*

The U.S. Small Business Administration offers help for small businesses. To find out about their offerings and publications, write to SBA Publications, PO Box 30, Denver, CO 80201-0030. Ask for SBA form 115A.

Further Reading:

Homemade Money, by Barbara Brabec, (Betterway Books).

How To Start A Business Without Quitting Your Job: The Moonlight Entrepreneurs Guide, by Philip Holland, (Ten Speed Press).

1001 Jobs You Can Start From Home, by Daryl Allen Hall, (John Wiley & Sons).

Working From Home, by Paul and Sara Edward's, (Tarcher).

HOME-BUYING AND MAINTENANCE

The following pamphlets are available from the Consumer Information Center, Pueblo CO 81009. Some of the booklets are free, others are available for a nominal charge. Send to the address above and request by item number and title. If there is a fee, include a check with your order.

Consumer Handbook on Adjustable Rate Mortgages. Describes basic features, advantages, risks and terminology. Explains how ARM's work and how to reduce your risks. 25 pages, items 331D. 50 cents.

A Consumer's Guide to Mortgage Lock-Ins. This 14 page booklet features basic information to help you obtain the terms of credit you want. Lists questions to ask when shopping for a mortgage. Item 332D. 50 cents.

A Consumer's Guide to Mortgage Refinancing. Learn the costs and how to tell if the time is right to refinance. This 8 page brochure is available for .50 cents. Item 333D.

Guide to Single Family Home Mortgage Insurance. FHA insurance protects lenders against losses on mortgages so they can offer you more generous terms. Learn what the costs, conditions and options are. This 21 page booklet is available for $1.25. Item 120D.

Home Buyer's Vocabulary. Brush up on the terminology of home-buying and real estate. This 14 page booklet is available for $1.00 Item 121D.

How to Buy a Home With a Low Down Payment. There are private and federal options for obtaining a mortgage. Learn how to qualify, determine what you can afford and more. This 12 page booklet is free. Item 574D.

The HUD Homebuying Guide. Here are step-by-step instructions for finding and financing a HUD home. Includes charts to help you estimate mortgage payments. This 11 page booklet is free. Item 575D.

Fixing Up Your Home and How to Finance It. This 2 page brochure offers information about hiring a contractor or doing the work yourself and the Title 1 loan program. Item 319D is available for .50 cents.

Keeping Your Home Safe. Use the crime-stoppers' checklist and other practical tips to protect your home from fire and theft. 13 pages. Item 627D. Free.

HOME EQUITY

When Your Home Is On the Line. Your home serves as collateral for a home equity loan. Here are questions, terms, tips, a checklist and more all to help you find the plan that best meets your particular needs. 16 pages. Item 336D is available for .50 cents.

INSURANCE QUESTIONS AND INFORMATION

For general insurance questions, contact the National Insurance Consumer Help line 800-942-4242

INVESTMENT INFORMATION

The National Association of Investors Corporation is a nonprofit organization that offers financial advice and information to individual investors. Contact 810-583-6242.

American Association of Individual Investors is a nonprofit organization that offers financial advice. Contact 800-428-2244

The following brochures are available for .50 cents each from the Consumer Information Center. Mail your requests to: Consumer Information Center, Pueblo, CO 81009.

An Introduction to Mutual Funds. Explains what they are, how to compare them, what factors to consider before investing and how to avoid common pitfalls. 15 pages. Request 353D.

Invest Wisely. Basic tips to help you select a brokerage firm and representative, make and monitor an investment, questions to ask and signs of problems. 14 pages. 354D.

KIDS AND MONEY

Kids, Cash, Plastic and You offers tips and activities to teach young children about money. It also offers information on allowances and how to help children make saving and spending decisions. Request booklet 657D from the Consumer Information Center, Pueblo, CO 81009.

LIFE INSURANCE

What You Should Know About Buying Life Insurance is a 23 page brochure free for the asking. Request booklet number 595D from the Consumer Information Center, Pueblo, CO 81009.

MONEY-SAVING RESOURCES

The Single Parents Money Guide by Emily Card with Christine Watts Kelly (Macmillan). Also be sure to visit Emily's web site which is full of tips and ideas at *http://www.womenmoney.com*

Send a self-addressed-stamped-envelope for a free sample copy of the *Cheapskate Monthly*, PO Box 2135, Paramount, CA 90273-8135 or visit them on the web at *http://www.cheapsk8.com*

Send a self-addressed-stamped-envelope with two first class stamps to *The Frugal Gazette Newsletter*, PO Box 3395, Newton, CT 06740-3395 or visit them on the web at *http://www.frugalgazette.com*

RETIREMENT

The following brochures are several of the many available from the Consumer Information Center. Mail your requests to: Consumer Information Center, Pueblo CO, 81009.

- *An Annuities brochure* offers 11 pages of detailed information on different types of annuities that can accumulate and generate retirement income. Includes a helpful quiz and questions to ask. Request brochure number 586D.
- *A brochure on 401(K)* Plans describes various investment options and plan features that you should discuss with your employers. This 14 page booklet is free for the asking. Request booklet number 655D.
- *Top Ten Ways to Beat the Clock and Prepare for Retirement* gives practical tips to help build your retirement savings, and resources for more information. This 2 page booklet is free. Request booklet number 594D.

Scudder offers a great *Retirement Planning Worksheet*. Visit their web site at *http://funds.scudder.com/* From their home page choose "Interactive Worksheets."

SOCIAL SECURITY

The following two brochures are available free. Mail your requests to the Consumer Information Center, Pueblo CO 81009.

Basic Facts on Social Security explains the different kind of Social Security benefits, who receives them and how they're financed.

Social Security: Understanding The Benefits explains retirement, disability, survivor's benefits, Medicare coverage, Supplemental Security Income and more.

CHAPTER SIX
TRANSFORMING DIFFICULT EMOTIONS INTO OPPORTUNITIES FOR GROWTH

If there are people on this planet with more demanding jobs or tougher emotions to cope with than single parents, we've never heard of them! The task of learning to deal with anger, stress, fatigue and other emotions, ranked as the number two challenge of single parents. Between dealing with an emotional past, an uncertain future and day-to-day demands, it's no wonder many parents feel emotionally challenged by the strength needed to cope.

Understanding emotions, and their underlying causes and

> Build in time to mourn the losses; becoming a single parent takes tremendous energy and the grieving process can get sidetracked.
>
> *D. Skeele*
> *Silver Spring, Maryland*

purposes, can offer a freedom to handle and deal with them more effectively.

CONFRONTING THE PAST

Many single parents reported that they had never fully accepted or found closure with their failed relationship. This open door can cause heartache, frustration and anger. No matter how long it's been since your entry into single parenthood, it is never to late to go back and find closure with the past.

There is a psychological process for dealing with the past that advances through several stages. The first is a period of mourning.

> Don't give up when all seems lost. Keep a positive outlook on life, it really helps and can make the difference in getting through the hard times. Persistence pays off.
>
> *Carol Goldberg Maeder*
> *Glen Mills, Pennsylvania*

ALLOWING TIME FOR LETTING GO
THE LOSS OF COMPANIONSHIP

It is important to allow yourself a mourning period for the loss of your partner. Even if the relationship had grown bitter or angry, there is still a need for mourning. At one point, the relationship contained the promise of companionship, shared hopes and dreams, and the pathway to a more fulfilled life. As the relationship ends, these dreams end with it.

For those who are still in love with their partner and having a relationship ended against their wishes, the mourning period takes on additional challenges. It involves the added task of accepting that the partner is not satisfied in the relationship and separating this from an opinion of your own self-worth. With children involved, contact with the other parent often continues. This contact becomes easier when there is a level of acceptance. This takes time, and it takes tears—and it takes faith that everything will indeed work itself out.

As you mourn, allow yourself to cry. Allow yourself to lock yourself in a room and be angry and bitter about the life you wanted that now is not. Don't bottle your feelings inside or insist on always being strong. Let the anger out. Let the pain out. Let the frustration out.

Notice the feelings that surface during this period. Are they mostly anger? Frustration? Rejection? Loneliness? These are the areas you will need to focus on when it comes time to move forward.

Mourning the loss of a relationship takes some people months and others years. There is no time limit for the mourning process. Yet, if you notice your mourning is hindering your relationships with friends and family, your children, your work performance, or your physical or mental health, for more than two to four weeks, you should seek help with a professional counselor. During traumas in our lives, it is common for depression to surface—especially in women. A short down period can quickly escalate into a major depression. While you may feel alone, hurt and like no one will understand, there are people who will. There are people who do.

Reach out. There is no need to go through any more hard times alone.

> If you are upset about being a single parent, do not allow it to ruin your life. Being a parent, single or not, has turned out to be the best thing I have ever done. While I loved my child's father very much, once I quit worrying about him and got on with my own and my child's life, I found a new love in my child that I never thought was possible.
>
> *Melissa Thomas*
> *Cincinnati, Ohio*

THE LOSS OF THE TWO-PARENT FORM

It is important to separate grieving the loss of a failed relationship from the loss of a failed family. Many single parents feel that a failed relationship equals a failed family and that society perceives them the same way. As Janice Molgen of the Coalition for Single Parents Day so beautifully states, "Where there is love, there is no such thing as a broken home."

It's fine to grieve the loss of the once traditional two-parent family, but don't let that fool you into thinking that you are any less of a family now. If you are riddled with feelings of failure, discuss them openly with a support group. Remember that the US Bureau of the Census estimates that 61% of children will spend part or all of their formative years in a single-parent family. The single-parent family may not be at all as "untraditional" as you believed. Perhaps you don't need to think of your family form as failed or unusual, but the norm and traditional. Whatever it takes, recognize that whether there is one parent or two, one child or ten, where there is love, there is family. It's a simple recipe.

KEEPING A JOURNAL

Throughout our lives, writing often becomes a chore instead of a reward. Writing for work or school takes all the pleasure from it, and the thought of picking up a pen on the road to self-discovery may not sound too enticing. But try it for a month. Or a week. For whatever length of time, record your feelings, write out your concerns, fears, dreams, days and memories. A journal can offer a great release and can serve as a valuable growing tool as time goes on.

> Being a single parent doesn't mean you have to do it alone, just that the team might be a bit smaller than most.
>
> *Dan Jacobwitz*
> *Bellrose, New York*

BECOMING SINGLE

Becoming single is the next task to conquer as you move through the psychological stages of an ending relationship. While with another person, many times our identities mesh into one. We might share the same friends, the same interests, hobbies and club memberships, the same group interests and more. The town you lived in might carry many memories of things once done together or people once visited as a couple.

As a relationship ends, we need to define ourselves in terms of who we are. Who are we without another person? Which people remain our friends? What changes occur in our lives now that we are no longer a wife or a husband or a significant other? Learning to look at your life and circumstances through the glasses of a single person instead of a committed partner is the second step to creating a healthy single lifestyle.

RESOLVING TOUGH EMOTIONS

Remember the emotions that surfaced as you mourned the passing of your relationship? Dealing with those is the next step to a successful and healthy life after relationship. Emotions that are left buried can resurface and cause immense damage down the road, often in ways we may not recognize.

For example, one single parent I know is angry with his wife for her behavior. Because of this, he often refuses her extra visitation even if the kids want to go. He justifies it by suddenly making other plans for the children or deeming the activity of the mother unsafe. While in some cases this might be good parenting, it's not in his case. He is acting out of his anger toward the other parent through the kids. While this does succeed in hurting the mother, it has one serious repercussion—the pain inflicted on the children.

Remember the pain and hurt involved in ending a relationship is your cross to bear; don't make it that of your children. They deserve the best family life possible. Part of that life is created by dealing with your unfinished business and helping to create a healthy environment.

Read books on the emotions that plague you. Talk about them at a single-parent support group. Take advantage of organizations that exist to help you. Learn to recognize the emotions that surface and develop healthy ways of dealing with them.

> It is okay and healthy to have your own "life" and activities as well as the ones you build with your chlid(ren).
> *Teri McCarthy*
> *Newark, California*

DEALING WITH THE ANGER

Throughout our upbringing, we are often taught that expressing anger is undesirable. Often we learn to bottle our hurt within us, scared to express feelings that we may find frightening ourselves.

Anger is healthy and natural and part of the healing process. Holding your anger within will only delay the process of healing. Bottled up anger can also lead to higher stress levels, unhealthy indirect behavior (that you may not even know is a result of the anger), depression and low self-esteem.

In the process of hiding our anger, we may say that we are "hurt" or "sad" rather than "angry," because feeling these emotions is often more acceptable to people. It's important to know that being angry is natural and normal.

> Try to make this situation a learning situation or a growing process. Instead of the end, make it a new beginning.
> *Sandy Miller*
> *Divorce Anonymous*
> *Facilitator,*
> *Michigan*

Here are some keys for handling the anger within your life:

Recognize what's happening.

The next time that you become angry, recognize the emotion when it occurs. Realize that you are getting angry and notice what is causing the transformation. Express your feelings honestly to whomever is involved. By confronting our anger at the time it occurs, we not only release it, but we also avoid miscommunication.

Get it out. If you find yourself angry with no means to express it, or upset about a time from your past, try a physical activity to exert your energy.

If you have been suffering from pent up emotions for some time, you may have a hard time identifying what makes you angry. Discuss your anger with a friend or hold a conversation with yourself. Ask yourself tough questions until you can uncover the source of tough emotions.

TAKING RESPONSIBILITY FOR OUR EMOTIONS

Know that you deserve happiness, peace and trust in your life.
Single Mother
Bathe, Maine

Modern society has become accustomed to blaming misfortunes on external circumstances or events. Just turn on the news or read the papers to spot people blaming others or the world at large for their problems. In a few cases this is warranted, but often blaming others is just an externalization so we don't have to take responsibility for our own lives and emotions.

People avoid taking responsibility because it's tough. It's easier to blame external sources than to realize we have the power within us to change. Once we commit to taking responsibility, we commit to change, and to taking control of our lives. It's a commitment that can cause fear, but that also has rewards.

To take responsibility, we must first admit that we had something to do with the hurt, anger and sadness that has occurred in our lives. Whatever our role, we must admit we played a part. Likewise, we need to notice the role we played in the times we were both happy and fulfilled. Own your emotions. Accept them. Learn to work with them, understand them and let them guide you to further self-awareness and understanding.

Believe in your ability and value as a parent and a family. The structure of the family is not the important thing, the parenting skills are what's important.

Sheridan Massey
Australia

THE COURAGE TO BEGIN AGAIN

Forming trusting, caring, adult relationships is the next step to rebuilding a healthy outlook as a single adult. These may be intimate relationships or close friendships. They may happen quickly or take several years. What is important is not to let one experience cause you to generalize about all others. It's fine to love being single and need little companionship in one's life. If, however, you crave more companionship and are held back by fear due to your past relationships, that needs to be dealt with.

A professional is a great springboard for talking about relationships. Identifying your weaknesses in a relationship to a trained ear can help greatly. Discuss what makes you happy. Identify what you would seek ideally in a future partner. Learn what negative patterns you engage in or allow others to inflict upon you. Learn about yourself, the way you love and the way you want to be loved. In a time of loneliness, some single parents report they remarry or move in with someone out of loneliness more than any other reason. This might account for why the rate of divorce for second marriages increases significantly. Instead of succumbing to this pitfall of loneliness, seek help so that your next relationship has a better chance of being healthy and rewarding.

> No matter how hard it is in the beginning, it will get better.
> *Charlotte Smith*
> *Enfield, Connecticut*

Healthy relationships with healthy boundaries are important with family members, friends and intimates. Use your last relationship as a springboard to learn more about how to make your next relationship—and all your relationships—more positive, rewarding and healthy.

RELIEVING THE DAY-TO-DAY
EMOTIONS OF SINGLE-PARENTING
FATIGUE

Exhaustion is a condition that plagues many of our survey respondents. With all the running around required from single parents, it's no wonder many feel tired and lost at times. With the high-stress, fast-paced requirements of single-parent life, it is important to minimize conditions that cause fatigue. Try these tactics to eliminate tired days:

Learn stress management. When a person is feeling stressed, his muscles are more tense and his body uses more energy. Consider taking a workshop, talking to a professional or reading a book on stress management. (See next page for details.)

Make sure that you are getting enough sleep. If you are putting in eight hours of sleep time but still waking feeling less than rejuvenated watch for slumber-inhibitors. Eat a lighter dinner. Avoid caffeine and other stimulants for at least four hours prior to bedtime, longer if possible.

Exercising 3-5 days a week, for 30 minutes or more, is a great way to increase your energy level. While it may seem you cannot spare thirty minutes, you will have more productive time and be more energetic if you incorporate regular exercise into your schedule. With this newfound energy, making up the time spent on exercising will be a snap. Many gyms now have day care. Or better yet, involve your child in the activity. Jogging strollers and bike attachments are perfect for toddlers. Try a bicycle for two, a long walk or lap at the pool with older children. This helps create quality time, increases self-esteem and energy, while teaching your child the benefits of taking care of himself. What a tradeoff for a 1½ to 2½ hour investment of your time each week.

Watch what you eat and when. Lunches that are high in carbohydrates serve as great pick-me-ups for a couple of hours, but lead to an afternoon slump. Eat a lunch high in protein to avoid the afternoon lull. Also avoid eating after seven p.m., if possible.

Be careful of dehydration. When you become thirsty, your body might be dehydrated. This is a common cause of fatigue. Attempt to drink eight to ten glasses of water each day.

Watch your weight. If you are more than ten pounds overweight, consider making preparations to switch to a more healthy eating regimen. Excess weight leads to fatigue.

STRESS

Whether it's induced by too little time, too much to do, family commitments or disagreements at work—stress is the buzzword of the decade. From headaches to ulcers to heart disease, everything can be blamed on this syndrome that has taken over today's men, women and children. Try the following relievers the next time stress has got you down:

Take a day off. Use a vacation day for a day to yourself. Resist the temptation to pack it full with all the things you "should do" to catch up. Instead do something you really enjoy. Take a road trip and crank the music, read a good book or have a movie marathon.

> I've been searching for all the "right" answers and no one seems to have them. I'm finally beginning to listen to my heart, follow where it leads and feel confident about my decisions.
> *Rachelle Faherty*
> *Roseville, California*

Give up always being right. Of course it would be wonderful if everything always went our way—but that just isn't possible. Have cooperation as your goal and let confrontations slip away. Remember that always being right equals more chances for a fight. Let go of high expectations and encourage give and take in all aspects of your life.

Give up the guilt. Guilt is a learned emotion. After parents, teachers and adults hound us with "shoulds" and "coulds," we learn to feel guilty and hold many of our mishaps against ourselves. While some guilt is necessary to keep a conscience, most of us carry around far more than our share. Learn to let go of the guilt, it doesn't offer any benefit and hurts no one but yourself.

If you find you cannot let go of the guilt, then indulge in it. Take twenty minutes and think of everything you want to feel guilty about. Get wild with it. Make everything your fault. Then take a deep breath and let it go. After giving in to the guilt, work on letting go.

Ask for help. When there is too much to do, call a friend and ask for help. Create a help list before you need it. Ask friends or relatives if you can call on them should you find yourself in a bind.

Squeeze ten minutes out of your sleep time to awake each morning and lay quietly. Think about the day ahead or daydream a little as you collect your thoughts.

Breathe. One of the quickest combatants for warding off stress is a few deep breaths. Place one hand on your stomach and focus on breathing from your stomach instead of your chest. Close your eyes and inhale for the count of ten. Then, exhale for the count of ten. Repeat five to ten times for a quick escape from stress.

Learning to successfully deal with emotions from our past, as well as dealing with new emotions arising from current situations, is key to living a balanced life. Invest time into nurturing your family's base asset—you.

MORE WORDS OF WISDOM FROM SINGLE PARENTS

"You can sometimes be a better parent by removing yourself temporarily from a stressful situation. Retreat to a private spot for a few minutes to collect yourself."

> *Single Mother*
> *Chicago, Illinois*

"You must learn to communicate, express your emotions and evaluate your marriage, courtship, upbringing, etc. This doesn't come easy. It's a lot of hard work, but it's the only way to make things work. The pain you experience is part of a growth process. You can't grow until you know where you are coming from. Knowing where you are coming from, then you have a choice of whether to break the cycle and change or not. Change is healthy."

> *Michael J. Roy*
> *Custodial father of three children*
> *Cambridge, Ontario, Canada*

"Pray, prepare and persevere."

> *N. Dolberry*
> *Orlando, Florida*

RESOURCES FOR TRANSFORMING DIFFICULT EMOTIONS

DIVORCE

THE DIVORCE RESOURCE NETWORK

The Divorce Resource Network was founded in 1991 by Pamela D. Blair (psychotherapist, Interfaith Minister, journalist, divorced and remarried mother of three children) in response to a growing public need to identify avenues for healing and help for families and individuals during the crisis and aftermath of divorce. The Network, where possible, provides counseling and referral assistance to those going through this painful life transition.

The Network is comprised of professionals and others who have offered and demonstrated compassion, skill and understanding to those experiencing divorce (i.e. therapists of many kinds, divorce attorneys and mediators, authors, career counselors, image consultants, forensic specialists and business owners, among others).

Since April 1994, the Network has published a monthly newsletter called *Surviving Divorce: A Newsletter to Support Women & Men in Transition.*

For further information and a sample copy of the newsletter call (914) 741-1044 or fax (914) 741-6232. Or write to Divorce Resource Network, PO Box 231, Hawthorne, NY 10532. E-mail *pamblair@aol.com*

Divorce magazine is a publication designed to help people cope with this difficult transition. Experts in the areas of family law, finances, mediation, real estate, relationships, children's issues and Emotional and physical health offer advice. A one year subscription is $9.95. Write to: *Divorce* Magazine, 145 Front St., E., #301, Toronto, Ontario, Canada M5A 1E3.

Vicki Lansky's Divorce Book For Parents. This is the best book we've found on divorce. If you are going through a divorce, pick up a copy for guidance on custody, how to tell the children and much more. Order at your local bookstore or order direct from Book Peddlers by calling (800) 255-3379. The cost is $5.99 plus $2.75 shipping and handling.

INFORMATION ON DEPRESSION

National Foundation for Depressive Illness offers a recorded announcement of the symptoms of depression and how to obtain help. (800) 239-1295

Depression Awareness   (800) 421-4211

National Depressive and Manic-Depressive Association "offers helpful information from advocacy to support. This not-for-profit organization was established to educate patients, families, mental health professionals and the general public concerning the nature and management of depressive and manic-depressive illness as treatable medial diseases." They foster self-help for parents and families and work to improve access to care. Their goals are carried out through a global network of 275 chapters and support groups. An individual membership is $20 and new members automatically receive a copy of *A Guide to Depressive and Manic-Depressive Illness: Diagnosis, Treatment and Support*, a bookstore catalog and a chapter directory. For a membership form or more information contact, National DMDA, 730 N. Franklin Street, Suite 501, Chicago, IL 60610-3526. Or print out the order form from their web site at *http://www.ndmda.org/Membership.htm* While you are there make sure to check out all the other information offered on the home page at *http://www.ndmda.org/*

The following free brochures are available from the Consumer Information Center. Send your request to: Consumer Information Center, Pueblo, CO 81009.

Plain Talk About Depression. Depression has many symptoms. This free brochure explains how it is diagnosed, treated and how to get help. Item 573D.

Panic Disorder. This brochure details what to do when anxiety or sudden fear seems too much to handle. Item 572D.

Obsessive-Compulsive Disorders. This brochure offers help and information for those suffering from repetitive thoughts and behaviors. Request item 571D.

Anxiety Disorders. Treatments available and resources to contact for more information on panic phobias, stress, obsessive-compulsive and other disorders. This 24 page booklet is free. Item 576D.

Biopolar Disorder (Manic-Depressive Illness). This free brochure details signs, symptoms and available treatments along with resources for how to get help. Item 568D.

Helping the Depressed Person Get Treatment. This free brochure gives specific advice and examples of symptoms and treatments to help depression. Item 569D.

GRIEF & LOSS

Grief Recovery Institute   (800) 445-4808

Funeral.Net offers a wealth of online bereavement resources. Some of the 40 or so listed resources include: support for young parents, sharing with others, children and grief, after loss, grief resources, teenage grief and more. Visit their web page at
http://www.funeral.net/info/brvres.html

WIDOWS AND WIDOWERS SUPPORT

WidowNet offers an online forum with information about widow/ers, grief books, support groups and much more. Visit their web site at:
http://www.fortnet.org/WidowNet/

To Live Again is a mutual help organization for widowed women supporting one another through the grief cycle. For information, write: To Live Again, PO Box 415, Springfield, PA 19064.

THEOS International Foundation is "dedicated to helping widowed people move successfully through the stages of grief and rebuild their lives through self-development and support groups." Widowed persons can request a general information packet by writing to: THEOS International Foundation, 322 Boulevard of the Allies, Pittsburgh, PA 15222-1919. Or call (412) 471-7779, Professional information packets are also available free of charge from the Pittsburgh address.

MENTAL HEALTH

National Mental Health Association	(800) 969-6642
National Clearinghouse Family Support	
Children's Mental Health	(800) 654-1247
Panic Disorder Information Hotline	(800) 64-PANIC

SELF-HELP CLEARINGHOUSES

Contact these numbers if you are looking for information on an illness, addiction, parenting or other stressful situation for which you cannot find a resource.

American Self-Help Clearinghouse	(201) 625-7101
National Mental Health Consumer's Self-Help Clearinghouse	
	(800) 553- 4539
National Self-Help Clearinghouse	(212) 354-8525
Clearinghouses in Canada -	
Toronto	(416) 487-4355
Vancouver	(604) 876-6086
Calgary	(403) 262-1117

CHAPTER SEVEN
CREATING A
SUPPORT NETWORK

"Learn to recognize when you need help and ask for it. It is our job to tap into the resources available to us. If something is not going right, help won't come to your door. Get books, go to classes, get counseling, go online—your child is more important than your pride. If you don't find what you need, keep looking. Demand what you need from someone who can change things or become an agent of change yourself."

Tracy Brant
Reading, Pennsylvania

With the escalation of single-parent families, support groups and other resources have sprouted up across the nation. Loneliness and isolation were two emotions commonly reported in our survey. Meeting the challenges of child-raising, house-management, work, decision-making and more—it's no wonder single parents are rightfully seeking support.

The majority of single parents who felt comfortable with life as a single parent were actively involved, or had been, with one or more support groups. By joining forces with other single parents, a person can find support, encouragement and reassurance at times when they are needed most—not to mention the satisfaction of helping and sharing with others.

Lack of time is the key reason many parents were not involved in a group. With hectic demands some parents couldn't find an hour to carve from their schedule. Availability was another issue, with many people reporting they did not know of a local group.

> When others offer to help you, accept their help. You may not ever be able to repay that particular person's kindness, but repay that person by helping someone else when you are in the position.
>
> *Single Mother*
> *Chicago, Illinois*

In this chapter we'll explore existing groups, how to start your own group and support groups for children. Locating and becoming involved with a group requires some homework. The payoff can be a shoulder to lean on and a hand to hold when days becomes overwhelming.

EXISTING SUPPORT GROUPS

Existing groups offer the quickest avenue for help. Many have chapters nationwide or, if support isn't available, you can start your own chapter with the aid of the parent organization. Parents Without Partners and The Single Parents Association are two such groups. See the resource section of this chapter for contact information and additional organizations.

CREATING YOUR OWN SUPPORT GROUP

With over 13 million single parents, one might guess these parents would be an easy group to locate. But as you know, single parents are some of the busiest individuals on this earth.

Many single parents are seeking support but just don't know where to look. Organizing your own support group can help you meet your own needs for single-parent companionship while also helping other single parents in your community.

The first step in creating a support group is to brainstorm and decide on the group's purpose. Different groups specialize in different areas. Some single-parent groups serve mostly as a place for families to meet, while others focus more on just adult meetings. Other single-parent groups work around a focused schedule that offers both support and socializing.

Take a moment to brainstorm and write down what your goals for a single parent group are. It is recommended that you not try to cover all areas equally. Choose one primary purpose for your group. Consider covering other areas to a lesser extent.

After you have a sketch of how you would like your group to be, it's time to narrow down some specifics. Consider the following:

Size - It's a good idea to have a vision of the number of members you would like. Some single parents are looking for a small group of adults to share their time with, while others are seeking large groups. Write down the ideal number of single parents you envision belonging to your group.

Meeting Schedules - How often will your group meet? Weekly? Biweekly? Monthly? Will the parents meet weekly with an optional "family day" one weekend each month? Think through your plans and time allowance as you form a tentative schedule of meetings. (It's best to create your plan on a calendar so you can sketch in the basics for founding the group on a timeline.) As the group forms, and you are unsure of how often to meet, you can discuss this amongst members or take a vote.

> After you've been to hell and back, make yourself available as a support to others going through this. Not only are you able to help others but you will then be able to see how far you have come and that you are making it!
>
> *Carol Goldberg Maeder*
> *Glen Mills, Pennsylvania*

Where will the meetings be held? Once you have a tentative schedule of meetings, the next step is to decide where to hold them. For smaller groups a restaurant often works well. Many small groups meet for coffee in the evening, or they catch a quick cup before work one morning each week. For larger groups it works well to alternate homes. Have one or more baby-sitters depending on the number of children. Chip in to minimize baby-sitting costs and the time of dropping your child at a sitter's home.

Give yourself a name. Last but not least, don't forget to give your support group a name. This will be used for promotion and announcing the new group to local media.

These are the fundamental decisions to be made before starting or announcing your support group. As your group grows, there will be more things to consider and plan, but first let's look at a few places to find the future members of your support group.

FINDING MEMBERS

There are many venues for pursuing members for your group. Following are a few of the ideas that work best.

Begin with who you know. Make a list of single parents you know that may be interested in the group. (As you work through this section, it's handy to keep a pencil and paper handy to record any thoughts, ideas and people you think of as you go along.) Ask the parents on your list who they know, word of mouth goes a long way.

Find a support network of other single parents in your area. It is very important to be able to communicate with others who know what you're thinking, you're feeling, where you are, have been and will be. Often you can also get to know these people enough to exchange baby-sitting once a month or so. If there is no group already, start one. Take an ad out in the local paper, put up an ad at church, at your child's school, etc. There are probably more single parents around our own neighborhoods than any of us realize.

Sara Lederhos
Ft. Collins, Colorado

Create a flyer. If your child is in school or a daycare program, create a flyer and ask the school to distribute it to the children to take home. Include your "mission statement" for the group along with your name and the best times to contact you. A summary of your tentative plans and goals is an added benefit to the flyer. If you belong to a church, try to make an announcement at a Sunday service or supply a mention of the new group to be printed in the church newsletter.

Announce your group to the media. A news release is a great way to inform the community of your presence. Include a cover letter asking the paper, radio station or television station to give the group a mention. If you like, offer yourself for an interview about your goals for the support group.

BASIC MATERIALS FOR YOUR GROUP

As your group takes form, it will be time to develop some basic rules and responsibilities for members. After these procedures are established, it's a good idea to print each sheet and make a packet to give new members. You may choose to do these things before the group takes official form or to wait and let your "starter members" have input in developing these materials. Consider creating the following:

A Member List - Create a member list. Go beyond name, address and phone to include children's names, ages and birthdays; parent's occupation, etc. This can help people to familiarize themselves with

> Learn to listen to that small voice inside. It is your best guide. If you think there is something wrong, there probably is. If you think things are great, they probably are.
>
> *Kathy A. Eads*
> *Pasadena, Texas*

other members and to refresh their memory about who is who as the group increases in size.

A Newsletter - A newsletter is a great way to keep regular contact with members. An 8½ by 11 format, double sided, 1-2 pages works well. This is a good project to delegate out to a member who works well with desktop design. A bimonthly or monthly edition is usually sufficient. Use the newsletter to list group news, upcoming events, member news, input wanted and the like.

A Calendar - A monthly calendar of events, deadlines, etc. is another handy tool for members. This can be included in the newsletter.

GROUP BENEFITS

As you find members for your group, it is good to provide a list of benefits and offerings of your group. Of course before you can provide them, you need to create them! Here are suggestions for benefits that have worked well for other groups.

A Co-Op night out - Have each single parent sign up for a Friday night slumber party. On that Friday, they host the children of the other single parents at their home. If you have eight members, this would result in each single parent watching the children one Friday every two months. In return, each single parent would have seven Friday nights to themselves. If some children are with another parent on weekends, toy around with different days and ideas to make this work for your members.

> Seek counseling for yourself and your children. You need someone objective to help you sort out your feelings and do problem-solving. I have made the choice to let my 11-year-old son go live with his father in another state, a gut-wrenching decision. My family does not support me in this decision, and I sensed disapproval from some of my friends also. I truly believe this is the best thing for him no matter what others say.
>
> *Single Mother*
> *Denver, Colorado*

Who do you know? Speakers can be an added bonus to meetings. Try to get a speaker every four to six weeks. Pastors, teachers, counselors, social workers, authors, parenting experts, CPA's, etc., can offer great presentations on subjects of interest to single parents. You can also survey members about whom they might want to invite or what topics they are curious to learn more about.

A hand-it-down program - Create a list that includes the ages of each member's children. Make this list descending from oldest child to

CREATING A SUPPORT NETWORK

youngest. Ask each single parent to fill out a form if there is anything that they are looking for, i.e. clothes, toys, games, etc. Then when a single parent is giving some items away, she can consult the list and pass it on to someone within the group.

A library - As funds available to your single-parent group increase, consider starting a Parenting Library. Purchase books that will be of interest to single parents and offer them on loan. To begin the library before you have funds to buy books, ask each single parent to donate relevant books to the library. A list of titles can be provided in the newsletter.

Family Get-Togethers - Aim to hold a "family get-together" monthly or bi-monthly. Picnics at the park, field trips or other activities can be a great way for both the children and parents to socialize and bond.

> Don't panic. Know that the path you are supposed to take will become clear.
>
> *Karen Minot*
> *Lakewood, Colorado*

Cooking Co-Op - This is a fun activity and a big time-saver if you have single parents who live within close proximity of one another. Put interested members into groups of five. Assign each night, Monday through Friday, to one of the five single parents. On the specified night, that single parent is in charge of Dinner Delivery. They will make dinner, enough for all five families, and distribute it. This allows single parents to eat home cooked meals five nights a week while only hassling with preparation one night. (And children really enjoy being the delivery kid.) This can also reduce grocery bills since you can buy just the food supplies for one dish and make your purchase in bulk quantities.

To charge or not to charge? Most single parents who begin support groups do not think of charging annual dues. As you look over your plan, estimate your expenses to begin the group. Some expenses to consider: copying flyers to distribute for promotion, copying newsletters, cost of mailing, etc. You may want to charge minimal dues to cover these costs. If you want to stay away from charging a membership fee, try organizing annual fund-raisers. Each member can support the group by devoting time or resources to one or two of these fund-raisers.

Roles & Responsibilities - As your group grows, consider establishing a board. This may contain a president, activities director, marketing director (in charge of newsletters, calendars and promotion), a treasurer, etc. This is a good way to distribute the responsibilities. Vote for these positions each year.

Expand the newsletter - Consider selling local advertising in your newsletter as the circulation amongst members increases. Contact local businesses and offer low rates on both classified and space ads. Use this money to fund activities and put a percent into a special project fund, for example, a scholarship fund for a child from a single-parent home.

Fund-raisers - Consider hosting a "Corner Carnival" for kids. Dances, bake sales, group rummages or other activities can also raise money for your

> Get into counseling. No one goes through a divorce without some scars. If you don't take care of your wounds, you will only pass them on to your children.
> *Kathy A. Eads*
> *Pasadena, Texas*

support group. Again, use this money to fund additional activities and consider supporting other single parents and their children within the community.

A NEW WAVE OF SUPPORT

With the popularity of the Internet growing at a rapid rate, worlds of information and support networks are as close as the click of a mouse.

Chat groups, message boards and information galore are available through Cyberspace. This avenue is great for those caught in a time crunch or who need help quickly.

The resources section of this chapter contains some information on newsgroups and web pages. Visit *The Single Parent Resource* on the Internet for more links to our favorite single-parent sites. Our Internet address is *http://www.championpress.com* (You'll find a free newsletter and plenty of articles there!)

SINGLE PARENTS DAY

MARCH 21

At the urging of Parents Without Partners, Congress established March 21 as Single Parents Day in 1984. The day is still largely unrecognized by much of the nation. It's up to us to spread the word and cherish this day for single parents' hard won achievements.

SUPPORT FOR KIDS

Kids need support just as their parents do, but they are often unsure of how to step up and ask for it. Offering a hand to create a support network for your child is extremely valuable. Many kids will act as though they don't need support, or don't have feelings of confusion over their family form. While sometimes this is the case, often it's a cover because they don't want to hurt either parent by explaining their feelings. A support group of peers lets children reveal their fears, insecurities and anger in a safe environment. It also helps to build confidence in their family form, and most importantly, understanding.

Check with your school to find out what counseling or support networks are available. If none are available, discuss starting a peer group for children of single-parents.

If you belong to a support group, take stock of the children's ages. If there are several children within the same age group, consider starting a kids' group on the side. Provide a living room or a meeting area with single parents taking turns being on premises (but not in the same room) to chaperone. Some support groups have launched this right alongside their current group to also minimize baby-sitting expenses.

Identify the areas where you and your child need support and don't be shy in seeking it. We all have a right to support networks to help us through trying times and to share with during the good times.

RESOURCES FOR SINGLE-PARENT SUPPORT

Practical Parenting is a free catalog listing of Vicki Lansky's books available by mail. To request your free copy write to: Practical Parenting, 15245 Minnetonka Blvd., Minnetonka MN 55345. Visit their web site at *http://www.practicalparenting.com*

Mothers of Preschoolers, International, Inc. (MOPS) "is a Christian organization that offers encouragement and support for all mothers of young children through a radio program, newsletters, publishing and groups which meet." There are also MOPS groups for teens. For information on joining a MOPS group in your area or starting a MOPS group write to: MOPS, 1311 S. Clarkson Street, Denver CO 80210. They also have a web site *http://www.mops.org*

At-Home Dad is a quarterly newsletter published by Peter Baylies to provide connections and resources for the two million fathers who stay home with their children. Sections include Home Business, Kids Tips, Resources and At-Home Dad Network. For information send a SASE to 61 Brightwood Ave., North Andover, MA 01845.

National Association of Mothers' Centers "enables members to be effective in using their individual and collective knowledge and experience as a catalyst for personal and societal changes that benefit mothers and families." Contact them at (800) 645-3823 for general information about Mothers' Centers with a list of centers by state, or leave your name, address and phone if you are interested in information on how centers are started. Or write to National Association of Mothers' Centers, 64 Division Avenue, Levittown, NY 11756.

Full-Time Dads seeks to support and encourage men in their work as fathers. Offers interviews, regular feature columns, news, information, reviews and resources for and about fathers. For information write to: PO Box 577, Cumberland, ME 04021.

National Organization of Mothers of Twins Clubs, Inc. "was founded in 1960 for the purpose of promoting the special aspects of child development which relate specifically to multiple birth children. The single parent coordinator will send the single parent of multiples several informative brochures. They also provide a "Single Parent Sharing/Networking Program" to enable single parents to correspond with one another. Parents are matched with others in similar situations." For more information write to: Single Parent Coordinator, NOMOTC, Executive Office, PO Box 23188, Albuquerque, NM 87192-1188. Or call (800)243-2276. Or visit their web site at *http://nomotc.org*

Solo Parenting Alliance, located in Seattle, Washington, serves the Seattle and Greater King County area. They offer a program called Family Home Share, Mutual Support Groups, a Resource Center, a quarterly newsletter titled *Solo Connections* and a yearly calendar of special events. For information, write to: Solo Parenting Alliance, 139 23rd Ave. South, Seattle, WA 98144. Or call (206)720-1655, Fax (206)328-8658. Or E-mail *solo@accessone.com*

United Fathers of America "empowers, encourages and assists parents who want to remain actively involved with their children physically as well as financially. The program involves one-on-one consultations that take into account each unique family situation. Practical options and alternatives and proven strategies and tactics within the family law system are provided. They also assist the client in separating the legal issues from the emotional issues. Paralegal services, ongoing case management and organization are also included in membership. Should a client choose to retain a Family Law attorney, a referral will be provided on request." For more information send a self-addressed-stamped-envelope to United Fathers of America, Inc., 595 The City Drive, Suite 202, Orange, CA 92868.

American Fathers Coalition is the federal lobbying arm of the National Congress for Fathers and Children. Non-membership, all-volunteer organization. Represents 280 fathers' rights groups throughout the country. Promotes positive father-inclusive policies on a federal legislative level. Send inquiries to: 2000 Pennsylvania Ave. NW, Suite 148, Washington, DC 20006. Or call (202) FATHERS.

Dad-to-Dad was founded in January 1995 by Curtis Cooper. The organization offers at home fathers opportunities to get together through children's play groups, dad's-night-out dinners and monthly newsletters. For information write to: Dad-to-Dad, 120 Ashbrook Lane, Roswell, GA 30076.

Lavender Families Resource Network "provides information and referrals for lesbian, gay and bisexual parents and their children on issues of custody & visitation, child rearing, donor insemination, adoption & fostering, schools, newsletters and pamphlets." For more information write to: Lavender Families Resource Network, PO Box 21567, Seattle, WA 98111. Or leave a request on their voice mail system at (206) 325-2643.

Formerly Employed Mothers at the Leading Edge (FEMALE) "is a national nonprofit organization for women who have left the full-time paid work force to raise their children at home. It is an organization for all women in transition between paid employment and at-home motherhood. It is not about opposing mothers who work outside the home." Use a self-addressed-stamped-envelope to request one or more of the following: informational brochure, sample newsletter and a listing of FEMALE Chapters and contact information. FEMALE would like to emphasize that they extend their support and services to all members, regardless of their marital status. All women and parents are welcome to join FEMALE, whether or not they work. This invitation is extended to dads also, "although male members must understand that our services are geared towards women and their needs and addressed as such."

Single Parents Association "is an international, nonprofit organization devoted to providing educational opportunities and fun, family activities through our always increasing Chapter network." Contact them directly for more information and a sample newsletter, (800) 704-2102 or inside Arizona (602) 788-5511.

The Fathers' Resource Center "offers programs and services designed to educate, offer information, and provide referral services and support for men. Support Groups, Parenting Classes, Family Law Clinics, Workshops and more" are just a few of the many offerings this resource provides. For an informational brochure and membership information write to: Fathers' Resource Center, Loring Park Office Building, 430 Oak Grove Street, Suite B3, Minneapolis, MN 55403. Or fax (612)-874-1014.

Parent's Without Partners (PWP) has over 400 chapters and 63,000 members in the United States and Canada. To locate a group near you, call PWP at (312) 664-6610 or visit their web site which lists local chapters. *http://www.parentsplace.com/readroom/pwp* Or you can write to PWP at Parents Without Partners International, Inc., 401 North Michigan Avenue, Chicago, IL 60611-4267.

The National Organization of Single Mothers, Inc. (NOSM) "is a clearinghouse of information and network of support to single mothers. NOSM helps establish support groups nationwide and publishes a bimonthly newsletter, SingleMOTHER." For more information, write to: NOSM, PO Box 68, Midland, NC 28107-0068. Or call (704)-888-KIDS. Or visit their web site at
http://www.parentsplace.com/readroom/nosm/index.html

Founded in 1981, Single Mothers By Choice (SMC) is a national support network for women having children while not in a permanent relationship with a man. For information contact SMC, PO Box 1642, Gracie Square Station, New York, NY 10028. Or visit their web site at
http://www.parentsplace.com/readroom/smc/index.html

Divorce Support Inc., is a free service offering telephone support and help. While they are based in Chicago, their scope is national. Call (312) 286-4541.

Parents Anonymous (PA) "has a network of community-based organizations across the country. They are guided by professionals who help parents share their frustrations, build self-esteem and gain child-rearing skills. The organization provides these services free of charge." For more information, write to: Parents Anonymous, Inc., The National Organization, 675 West Foothill Boulevard, Suite 200, Claremont, CA 91711. Or call (909) 625-6184

National Parenting Association "is a nonprofit, nonpartisan organization dedicated to building a nationwide parents' movement that will unite a broad spectrum of American families. Our mission is to put the needs of America's 62 million parents at the top of the national agenda by making their voices heard in the voting booth, the schools, the workplace and the media. Working together with others who cherish children, we are committed to creating a nation that values and supports the critical role of mothers and fathers in shaping their children's future." For more information about NPA write to: National Parenting Association, 51 West 74th Street, Suite 1-B, New York, NY 10023. Or call (800) 709-8795.

National Children's Coalition has put together a wonderful resource on the Internet. The Youth & Children Resources Net offers a wide variety of links to organizations and resources of interest to parents. Visit their web site at *http://www.slip.net/~scmetro/childco.htm*

SUPPORT FOR KIDS

Big Brothers Big Sisters of America "is the oldest mentoring organization serving youth in the country. BBBSA has provided one-to-one mentoring relationships between adult volunteers and children at risk since 1904. BBBSA currently serves over 100,000 children and youth in more than 500 agencies throughout the United States." For more information contact your local agency or visit their web site at *http://www.bbbsa.org*

Rainbows "is a not-for-profit, international organization that offers training and curricula for establishing peer support groups in churches, synagogues, schools or social agencies. These curricula are available for children and adults of all ages and religious denominations who are grieving a death, divorce or any other painful transition in their family. Rainbows was created to provide children, adolescents and adults an opportunity for healing after their painful loss. Rainbows offers four age-directed curricula, Rainbows (elementary age edition), Spectrum (adolescent age edition), Kaleidoscope (college-age adult edition,) and Prism (single parent edition)." For more information contact Rainbows at 1111 Tower Road, Schaumburg, IL 60173. Or phone (800) 266-3206.

Kids' Turn is "a nonprofit agency to help children whose parents separate or divorce. This educational program for children and parents teaches family members the skills that can improve communication between child and parents, and helps parents understand their children's experience during and after divorce. The program also teaches children coping skills to help deal with the family's reorganization. The six-week program is designed for children ages 4-14. Currently the program is offered in the San Francisco area, Santa Rosa, Redding and soon in San Diego. Featured on the ABC-TV news program 20/20 in 1995, the program drew attention from many groups. The curriculum is now available for other not-for-profit groups who are interested in starting the program in their area. A videotape also offers clips of what occurs at a workshop." For more information, visit their web site at *http://members.aol.com/kidsturn/ index.html*, e-mail *KidsTurn@aol.com*, or write to Kid's Turn, 1242 Market Street, fourth floor, San Francisco, CA 94102.

ONLINE SUPPORT
USENET
Newsgroups can be a good source for posting questions and gaining feedback online. But user beware, newsgroups tend to have their own "personality," so it's best to observe and read the posts for a while before "jumping" in.

Some newsgroups to get you started include:

Alt.support.single-parents	Alt.child-support
Alt.support.divorce	misc.kids
soc.women	soc.men
Alt.support.step-parents	Alt.dads-rights

Sole Mothers International is an organization "that exists for the benefit and encouragement of single parents. Their mission is to provide resources and information to aid single parents with everyday challenges." They publish a quarterly newsletter for $6.00 a year and have an extensive web site with plenty of resources. Check it out at *http://home.navisoft.com/solemom/*

National Center for Fathering "champions the role of responsible fatherhood to our generation and equips and inspires men to be more engaged in the lives of children." To receive a free copy of the quarterly magazine, *Today's Father*, which contains ideas and practical tips for dads call (800) 593-3237. For more information, visit their web site at *http://www.fathers.com* or write to: National Center for Fathering, 10200 W. 75th, Suite 267, Shawnee Mission, KS 66204.

Moms Online defines itself as a home for Moms in cyberspace. With tips, chat and featured articles, this site is a great stop on your journey through cyberspace. Check it out at *http://www.momsonline.com/*

DivorceCare offers "a series of support groups conducted by people who understand what you are experiencing. You'll learn how to deal with the pain of the past and look forward to rebuilding your life."

These non-denominational groups are open to everyone. To find a support group near you, access the support group finder on the Internet at *http://www.divorcecare.com/FNDR.html* or call (919) 571-7735.

divorcesource.com provides free articles and information on the financial, legal, psychological, real-estate and other aspects of divorce. There is also a Family Law Professional Directory for locating professional assistance near you. A thorough listing of support groups is also offered. Check out this valuable site at *http://www.divorcesource.com/*

Single Rose: Resource for Single Mothers, check out this well done site for articles, chat and subscription information.
http://www.singlerose.com

Divorce Online "is an electronic resource for people involved in, or facing the prospect of divorce. Divorce Online provides free articles and information on the financial, legal, psychological, real-estate and other aspects of divorce. Additionally, you can turn to the Professional Referral section of Divorce Online to locate professional assistance near you." Visit their web site at
http://www.divorce-online.com/

CHAPTER EIGHT
THE SOCIAL LIFE OF THE SINGLE PARENT

"You deserve another chance at a relationship when you are ready (and if you want one!) No matter what, you deserve to have someone special in your life besides your kids."

Single Mother
Detroit, Michigan

From friendship to companionship to remarriage, the social life of the single parent is one of the hardest areas to explore. This is primarily because there are no set rules or definitions. Each person and each family varies, and with so many of the issues being emotional-related, the "answers" depend greatly on where each family and its members reside emotionally.

Maintain relationships outside of the family to keep a perspective, receive positive, objective feedback, and just to take a break.

William Rathbun
Lavina, Montana

Let's look at some different types of adult interaction and issues that may arise.

ADULT ONE-ON-ONE INTERACTION

Of the participants in our survey, few went out with a friend or significant other on a regular basis (see survey findings in this section). Yet the value of these outings was confirmed by other single parents, many who mentioned how important it is to make time for one's self.

We know that adult one-on-one interaction is an important ingredient to successful single-parenting. This interaction allows you time to be a "person" as well as a parent, to rejuvenate, find help, counsel and friendship. Adult interaction is also vital to avoid the pitfall of relying too heavily on children to fill the gap left by an adult.

If you regularly set aside time for outings with friends, support groups or dates, you will reap the benefit. Once a week is a good goal for getting out, biweekly if that is out of the question. Whether you see a movie, spend a day shopping, take a walk, attend a support group, grab lunch or a coffee—try to make a resolution to give yourself adult interaction on a regular basis.

BEGINNING AGAIN

"How do I know if I'm ready to begin dating again?" is a question I frequently hear. Unfortunately there are no tip sheets, quizzes or point and shoot resolutions for this question. Each single parent must consider her unique emotional circumstances and those of the children as this decision is made.

> Take relationships slowly. It's frustrating when you're lonely, but if you move into a relationship too fast you can't be as objective as needed and the confusion you may present to your children makes their adjustments even more traumatic.
> *Single Mother*
> *Helena, Montana*

Every person is entitled to a relationship that offers rewards, growth and encouragement with another healthy adult. Finding this relationship, and being ready for this relationship, is a task each of us must tackle on our own. Likewise, there is nothing wrong with choosing to stay single. In fact, more and more people are doing just that. Again, it depends on how you feel, what your goals are, and where you are at emotionally. Before a new relationship is started, I recommend the following:

Know why you're looking. Are you seeking companionship out of loneliness or to enhance your life and to share with another person? Many people seek out another to ease their loneliness which puts an unneeded pressure on a relationship. Most successful relationships work because they contain two healthy people, both of whom can be independent of each other, and create a new dimension when they merge.

Know your goals. Have an idea of what you are looking for in companionship. What specific qualities do you find attractive? What specific qualities do you feel compliment you, your children and your lifestyle? What type of companionship are you seeking? Do you need a friend, someone to date or are you hoping to ultimately remarry? Having your goals firmly in mind will help you to relate them to new interests.

If two people are clearly seeking different needs from a relationship, there is little point in investing a lot of time in it. It's best to end the relationship before the hurt becomes worse down the line.

Face the past. Have you objectively looked at your past relationships and tried to learn why they didn't work? If communication was an issue, have you studied up on it or spoken with someone? If there was abuse or co-dependency, have you successfully worked through these issues to minimize your chances of seeking a similar relationship? Whatever the issues that contributed to the ending of your prior relationships, analyze and learn from them in detail before embarking on another.

CONSIDER THE CHILDREN

Think through the new relationship as it concerns your children. I have seen some single parents who refuse to date because it might upset the children. I don't believe this. I believe that single parents are entitled to fulfilling relationships, and that children should be considered but shouldn't control the decision of when or whether to date. It's true that careless dating or flaunting of romance can hurt children, so think through ahead of time how this might affect your children. Here are a few issues to consider:

Don't introduce your child to each person that you meet. Wait until you know if the relationship is going to be long term. A child will only be hurt and disappointed if she is repeatedly introduced to relationships that don't last long.

Make sure a new relationship does not cut too far into your child's time. Sometimes you may need to take your child with you, other times you may hire a sitter. Either way, make sure to still leave plenty of one-on-one time with your child. A new interest can leave a

---

SURVEY FINDINGS

We asked our survey participants how they felt about the following statements, "I feel confident and enjoy my life as a single parent." Here is what they said:

Five (strongly disagree)	10%
Four	15%
Three	24%
Two	26%
One (strongly agree)	22%
No opinion	3%

> After divorce, get your life back together and learn how to take care of yourself without having to depend on another before you get into another relationship.
>
> *Deborah Critzer*
> *Ventura, California*

child feeling threatened and fearful that she might lose your attention. Regular one-on-one time will help alleviate this concern.

How much time has passed? Has your child had the time and outlets to deal with his emotions over the divorce, separation or loss of a parent? Making sure kids have successfully dealt with their emotions can decrease anger and negative behavior directed toward you and your new interest.

Do you have good communication with your child? Are the lines of communication strong enough that your child would come to you if she were feeling threatened, unsure or concerned? Reassure your child that she always comes first and you are always willing to listen.

Not all of these issues will necessarily be resolved at the time you begin dating. Sometimes the answers come through experience. We may think we know what we want in a partner, only to discover the very qualities we *thought* we wanted aren't offering the fulfillment we had hoped for. Try to have an open mind about your needs, but be willing to revamp and regroup as you go along.

> Make sure that if you establish a relationship that your single parenting and its special needs are understood by the other person up front.
>
> *Jack White*
> *Lee, New Hampshire*

WHERE TO MEET PEOPLE

If you feel you are ready to meet new people but aren't sure where to begin, try the following:

- Join groups that share your interests.
- Join a singles group or watch for singles-only events.

- Let your friends know that you are considering dating again. Friends that know you well might have an idea of someone they would like you to meet.

- Consider placing a personal ad. More and more people are successfully finding relationships through personal ads. Browse the ads in your local paper or consider placing one yourself.

> Don't introduce your child to every person you date until you're reasonably sure the other person will be around awhile.
>
> *Mary J. Waddell*

- Check out Cyberspace. Unless you are in a relatively large city it might be hard to meet locals through the Internet. But the Internet does offer a playground of social interaction, single-parent camraderie and matchmaking; *http://www.match.com* is a good place to start.

WHAT ABOUT OVERNIGHT GUESTS?

This is a very personal issue for single parents, thus making it hard to offer a "one size fits all" answer. On the whole, I recommend avoiding overnight guests, unless (1) you have been with the person a long while; (2) your children are comfortable with the person; and (3) you expect the relationship to be long term. While it's nice to wake up with someone in your home and arms, the ramifications of this on your children serve as a strong deterrent.

Instead of confusing children, opt to have your "overnights" somewhere else. While children should know the basics of your social life, they do not need information on your sex life. Consider a weekend getaway or staying at your partner's residence on a

> If you meet people you'd like to know better, take the initiative and get their phone number or give yours.
>
> *Maria C. Kleinbub*
> *Maspeth, New York*

night when the children are at a friend's home or with the other parent. This won't always be convenient and there will be nights when you yearn to be held. It's okay to have your partner over and to let him stay late, just try to avoid your children wondering, "Who is sleeping in your bed?" or "Who is in the shower?"

By minimizing what your child is exposed to, you will minimize conflicts, objections and angry outbursts from your child.

> When dating again, always let the man or woman know that your children come first.
>
> *Tonia Dunn*
> *Raleigh, North Carolina*

I want to share the following piece with you. I printed it a while back in *The Single Parent Resource* and thought it summarized much of the single-parent social life perfectly. Courtesy of Lyn Worthen, here it is.

So We're Single Again
by Lyn Worthen

A friend of mine, a single father of two boisterous kindergartners, called me up the other day, absolutely beside himself with frustration. It seemed his girlfriend had decided to dump him because she couldn't handle the children.

"I understand you so much better now," he told me. (This is the same guy who several months previously had decided that my four children were too much for him to handle.)

I didn't laugh. I didn't say, "I told you so," or anything like that. I made a few suggestions to him about helping his girlfriend get used to the boys on their own turf rather than in her less than childproofed home, offered a few words of encouragement, and hung up.

Then I laughed. For a long time.

This whole dating thing was really much easier the first time around. At least it was for me. If someone invited me out for coffee on the way home from work, I didn't have to add a doubled or tripled daycare fee to the price of the drink.

Nor did I have to squeeze dates into my lunch hour to avoid such a complication.

Single people without children don't have this problem. They are stereotyped as free spirits who can come and go as they like, pretty much at the drop of a hat, and while I try to avoid thinking in stereotypes, all singles without kids I know pretty well fit the mold. They can invite a date into their homes without wondering whether or not World War III has occurred during their absence. They never have to kick aside piles of stuffed animals and half-eaten lunches. (Okay, so some of them do, but at least they knew they were there in the first place because it was their half-eaten lunch. Single parents never know what they're bringing a date into because they aren't the ones making the mess.)

Singles without children also fail to understand that there is never going to be a less hectic time to call you on the phone. They're generally used to long stretches of peace and quiet that they cover up by turning on the stereo or television; single parents, on the other hand, are used to long stretches of chaos that we cover up by turning on the stereo or television. So even when we turn down the mechanical noise to talk on the phone to a prospective date, the live noise continues. Singles without kids don't understand that this is normal, and I've had more than one person not call me back after hearing my children playing some harmless, but deafening, game in the background.

> If you want a relationship with someone again, keep your chin up and get involved in activities you like. If someone is meant to be in your life, they will accept you for who you are no matter the circumstances. If a relationship does not come your way, well, look at what a beautiful child you have and be thankful.
> *Karen Kilroy*
> *Holliston, Massachusetts*

So what do we do? Date strictly within the ranks of single parents? That's a thought worthy of consideration, but one that brings with it all the challenges facing blended families; which, while not insurmountable, are certainly not what I bargained for when I signed up for parenthood.

> Don't give up your life for your kids or anyone else.
> M. Bodden
> Brooklyn, New York

Or we could do what one friend of mine has done, and simply not tell our prospective partners that we have children until they're so head-over-heels for us that we hope they'll accept the children just because they're ours. That kind of game-playing may work for her, but it doesn't work for me.

I've taken to just being honest. When I meet someone who seems both interested and interesting, I let him know up front that I have children. I also let him know that I'm not interviewing for stepfathers right now. As an adult, I enjoy adult company, and if that should start to develop into an actual relationship, then, and only then, do the children become a factor. It weeds out a lot of potential disasters.

> If you have had an unsuccessful marriage, don't jump into another relationship right away until you really get to know yourself and get an idea of what you want and need from a partner.
> Single Mother
> Vancouver, B.C.

Sure, I don't go out as much as my friend does, but I don't get hurt as often, either. And neither do my kids.

Whether you choose to continue to sail solo or embark on a new relationship, be patient and take your time. Move slowly forward, with whatever decision, for your own sake and that of your children.

RESOURCES FOR THE SINGLE-PARENT SOCIAL LIFE

Single Again Magazine is published specifically for the divorced, separated and widowed, providing information for dealing with these changes and experiences. The magazine also includes articles on spirituality, health, finances, counseling and relationships, along with photo personals and public personals. For more information, visit their web site at *http://www.singleagain.com/order.htm* or write to

Scholl & Associates

Circulation Department

PO Box 3528

Fairfield, CA 94533

The Stepfamily Foundation Inc. "provides counseling, on the telephone and in person, and information to create a successful step relationship. Founded in 1975, the Stepfamily Foundation has

---

FACTS ON FLYING SOLO

from the Bureau of the Census

The number of married persons has increased from 95 million to 114.5 million between 1970 and 1993, although the increase in unmarried adults was greater (from 37.5 million to 72.6 million). The number of never-married persons doubled from 21.4 million to 42.3 million during the same time period, and accounted for the largest share of unmarried adults.

The number of unmarried-couple households was 3.5 million in 1993, seven times larger than the 523,000 unmarried-couple households in 1970.

Over the last two decades, the number of women living alone rose 94 percent (from 7.3 million to 14.2 million), while the number of men living alone rose 167 percent (from 3.5 to 9.4 million).

pioneered this particular method of counseling. We provide the vital training, information and counseling to avoid the pitfalls which often stress these relation-ships." Telephone counsel-

> Never use your children as an excuse for not having a social life.
> *Jill Steltenpohl*
> *Janesville, Wisconsin*

ing, intensive counseling and short model counseling are a few of the options available. For information on books, videos and membership, write to: Step Family Foundation, 333 West End Ave., New York, NY 10023. Or call (212) 877-3244. Or visit their web site at *http://www.stepfamily.org/counseling.html*

The New Intimacy - "No matter how much two people have in common, when they enter into a relationship their many differences soon become apparent. Most people are threatened by differences and so they pull back when they might have been able to have had a great relationship—if they only knew how to use those very same differences as the basis for deep intimacy. *The New Intimacy* by Judith Sherven, Ph.D., and James Sniechowski, Ph.D., shows the reader how to do that in very practical ways, including how to use the inevitable conflicts to get to know each other better, and how to resolve those conflicts in ways that strengthen and enrich the relationship. It's also a great blueprint for dealing with all the many ways your children are different from you—with respect and value for both you and your child." (Health Communications, Inc., $12.95.)

CHAPTER NINE

COMMITTING TO MAKING YOUR CUSTODIAL ARRANGEMENT WORK

Making custody work is vital to your own mental health and that of your children. Although the specific concern of "ensuring that my children have the opportunity to have a good relationship with the other parent" was a concern to only 42% of our participants, the emotional well-being of children ranked high. In addition, explaining a parent's absence is a topic 69% of survey participants want to see addressed. We will touch on all three of these areas in this chapter.

Throughout their childhood, children are dramatically and continually affected by how their parents interact with, and behave toward, each other. Since this is such an important area to children, we wanted to offer thorough coverage on how to make a custodial arrangement work.

"Work" can be defined differently for different families. Ideally it's where two parents communicate and work together (whether married or single) in order to best raise their children. With emotions running high after a separation or divorce we often intend to do what is best for the child, only to find that old feelings and past hurts can get in the way.

There are ways to minimize the conflicts and accentuate the positives of a working relationship. A strong commitment will be needed as you pave the way for a working relationship with your former partner. It's not always easy and it may take some time, but it's the best thing you can do for your child's benefit. And it's a great way to parent.

Let's look at some ways that you may begin carving a path for relationships that benefit everyone. NOTE: If the other parent is absent from your child's life, please see the section of this chapter titled, *Dealing With An Absent Parent.*

SURVEY FINDINGS

Of our survey participants for whom custodial arrangements were applicable, 53% were satisfied with their current arrangement, 46% were not satisfied. One percent had no opinion. Of those who were satisfied, the majority were those who shared joint custody or had a regular schedule established with the other parent. The majority of those who were least satisfied were custodial parents who reported non-custodial parents that did not see their children regularly. The majority of these custodial parents felt they would be satisfied if a regular schedule was established and upheld.

IT TAKES A COMMITMENT

Keeping perspective is the key to making a relationship with another parent work. Each parent must remember that this is being done for the child's benefit. While you and your ex may no longer be personally involved, a child has the right to remain involved in both parents' lives—provided he chooses to and it imposes no threat to his safety.

With emotions running high, it may be that one parent is ready to make a go of a working relationship, while the other parent is not. That's all right. Keep your head and heart focused on the well-being of your child as you forge ahead and pave the way for a productive parenting relationship. In time (sometimes more time than we might like) the other parent will usually come around. Remember never to fight fire with fire, or everyone will get burned, most of all, the child.

When things get rough or times are tense, focus on your child. Remember why you are doing this. By keeping your focus on the child, you will have more stamina to continue through rough times to a successful arrangement for all.

If you find yourself in a situation with a parent who is unwilling to practice a parenting partnership, go ahead and begin implementing what you can of these ideas. As the other parent sees how this can make life simpler while benefiting the child, she will most likely come around.

> Never take the other parent away from the children. The children will always want to know the other parent, and you will only be pushing yourself away, not the other parent. Let the children make up their own minds about the other parent.
> *Rochelle Hislar*
> *Santa Monica, California*

WEEKLY MEETINGS

When implementing the arrangements for a successful co-parenting endeavor, it is important to set clear boundaries. Part of the arrangement will require weekly meetings, whether they be in person or via phone. Later in this chapter, we'll look at specifics for conducting successful meetings.

To begin your parenting agreement, there are a few basics that should be covered at your first meeting. One of the most important and most beneficial to the children are house rules.

Many single parents complain that their co-parent does not follow similar rules. Sometimes the child gets extra toys, candy, doesn't have to do chores or is allowed to stay up late. While this may let the child admire the parent, in the long run, it's not best for the child.

Children need structure and schedules to thrive. They need to know that both parents have limits. Children need responsibilities.

Establish these as soon as possible and keep them consistent in both homes. Likewise, it is unrealistic to think that responsibilities will be exactly the same in both households. Aim for consistency, not an exact mirror of your own household.

Some basics to consider at the first meeting include:

Keep things comfortable. Make sure that your child has all the basic supplies at each household. She should have extra clothes, a toothbrush, etc. at each home. This allows each residence to feel like "home," instead of the child feeling like she is a "visitor."

Establish ground rules. Meet to establish a set of ground rules and consequences should they be broken. Once decided upon, put these rules in writing and explain them to your child.

> Remember that the other parent is mommy or daddy. Every word you utter about that person directly impacts your child, but seldom has any affect on the parent at all.
>
> *Alice Clearman Fusco*
> *Riverside, California*

Identify Responsibilities. If a child visits one parent for the weekend only, he should have a few less responsibilities so that he may maximize his time with the parent. Try to make responsibilities based on ratio, i.e. the child has one responsibility per day (unloading dishwasher, keeping room clean, etc.) Make the responsibilities fair at each household.

Establish the same bedtime at both households. This is an area where consistency counts. An over-tired child leads to an irritable child the next day.

Stay in touch. Both parents should be on the school mailing list to receive announcements, report cards and the like.

Stay informed. Each parent should have full knowledge of the medical history of the child. This includes: doses of over the counter and prescription medications, special health problems, known allergies, immunization schedules and any other relevant health concerns.

When a parent slips. If a parent slips on following the above guidelines, try not to let it upset you. Simply add it to your list of things to
discuss at your next meeting. Working together will require working
through some mistakes or mishaps. Keep your best foot forward and
your child will too.

Ten Keys For A Successful Working Relationship

- Keep parenting separate from your personal differences.
- Avoid too much personal inter-action so children do not develop reconciliation fantasies.
- Talk about all money and child-rearing matters in private.
- Develop an organized plan.
- Remember the good qualities in each other.
- Be fair and realistic about money and visitation matters.
- Let go. You each have your own life.
- Share parenting responsibilities and decisions.
- Respect, listen and consider each other's ideas.
- Encourage involvement.

> Don't allow the relation-
> ship between you and the
> other parent to affect the
> relationship between you
> and your child.
> *Single Mother*
> *Guilford, Maine*

SAMPLE AGENDA

It is a good idea to follow a pattern and agenda during your meetings.
Here is an example of one successful way to conduct a business
relationship.

1. Arrange a meeting time, preferably at the same time each week.
2. Confirm the meeting a day or two in advance.
3. Create an agenda of items to be discussed (see below example) and
   do not stray from the agenda.
4. After your meeting, summarize what was decided in a quick memo

and send it to the other parent by fax, e-mail or regular mail. Don't use the child to deliver these or any other materials—even if he offers.

Here are items to be discussed when meeting.

- Begin by briefing the other parent on news of the past week. This may include school developments, any new friends, interests or hobbies, nightmares, movies seen, etc.

- List any concerns that you, teachers or friends have had about the child.

- Discuss the activities for the upcoming week and any plans that might differ from the established schedule.

- Forecast upcoming holidays and trips that could affect the child's schedule.

- Make sure each parent is aware of upcoming school events such as conferences, sporting events, concerts and the like.

> Honor your child's relationship to the other parent. He or she loves him and it is important you are accepting of their love for the other parent.
>
> *Nancy Patmont*
> *Grass Valley,*
> *California*

- In addition to the above, establish a regular day to add additional items to the agenda. Do this a couple days prior to each meeting so that you can print the agenda and both have a copy to look over and think about before meeting.

GUIDELINES FOR
SUCCESSFUL PARENT MEETINGS

- Conduct meetings in a public place, like a restaurant or coffee shop. Think of this arrangement in terms of business and handle yourself professionally. This will be challenging at first, given what you've shared, but many single parents have made it work. It is also best to meet during a lunch hour or at another time when the meeting has a definite beginning and end. Most people get around an hour for lunch; this is ample time for your meeting. Avoid evening get-togethers where it's easy to linger after dinner and there is no definite time limit.

- Avoid the past. When you meet, avoid reminiscing or discussing times passed. Stay focused on the issues at hand—successfully raising your child(ren).

- Keep meetings away from children. Don't meet when your children are present and avoid phone conversations when children are within earshot. This will only confuse children about your relationship. Or, if conversation gets heated, children will be needlessly hurt.

- Always make an appointment. Unexpected phone calls should only happen during an emergency situation or something of utmost importance, otherwise all interactions should be scheduled.

At first this may sound a little cold or impersonal, but it's a matter of focusing on what is important—the children. If you choose to have a more friendly relationship with your former partner as time goes on, great. Though it's still best to keep calls away from the children so they don't get confused about your involvement or dream of a reconciliation that you don't have in your plans.

NOTES ON SPECIFIC TYPES OF CUSTODY

Although custody arrangements are finalized, smooth sailing from that point on isn't. With primary custody comes the dilemma of keeping the parent living outside the home involved in the children's lives. The parent who lives outside the home may be battling feelings of loneliness. He may wonder how to remain a part of his child's life without day-to-day, in-person interaction. This can be further complicated if miles separate a parent and child.

> Instead of a baby-sitter, when convenient, let the other parent spend the extra time with the children.
> *Single Mother*
> *New Orleans, Louisiana*

Parents who have a joint custody arrangement face the challenge of creating balance and similar rules between two households. They attempt this while trying to maintain a strong sense of security in both homes.

Unfortunately, there are no written guidelines to make these arrangements easier. Following are some ideas that can help. Not all of them will be applicable to your family form. Try the ideas that make the most sense for you.

> Be confident in your own abilities as a parent, regardless of what the other parent does or does not do for your child.
> *Single Mother*
> *Chicago, Illinois*

PRIMARY PHYSICAL CUSTODY
KEEPING THE OTHER PARENT INVOLVED

It's a difficult task to not let your feelings for your ex influence his visiting arrangements. Many times a parent is angry, hurt and resentful. Visitation can become a means of getting back at your ex-partner. Sometimes this is a conscious choice, but often it occurs subconsciously.

Your feelings aren't necessarily your child's. Your child has the right to form his own decisions and the right to see and love both of his parents. You can help by encouraging the other parent to remain in your child's life. Doing this isn't easy. It requires you to put your feelings aside and to focus on your child's needs.

Your encouragement is important. The non-custodial parent may be feeling cast aside, unneeded or unimportant. These feelings may cause him to not pursue a relationship with his children. Instead of waiting on him, try to encourage his involvement. Remember, you are focusing on your children now.

WAYS TO PROMOTE THE NON-CUSTODIAL
PARENT RELATIONSHIP

Don't ridicule. Children will often keep different hours or eat different things when with the other parent. Don't ridicule the other parent because her style of parenting is different. Instead, bite your tongue. Will staying up a couple of hours later on a weekend night do any permanent damage? No. If you ridicule the other parent, she may feel she is parenting "wrong" and eventually visits may begin to decrease. If the discrepancies are too major to be ignored, add these issues to the list of items to be discussed at a single-parent meeting between the two of you.

Try being flexible. If visits are rare, try to be a little more flexible in your visitation schedule to encourage increased visiting.

Discuss issues together. If your child is facing a problem in school, her social life or at home, let the other parent know. Think it through together. The other parent will be pleased to know that you value his opinion in parenting issues.

Keep the other parent posted. Send copies of report cards, drawings and graded papers on a regular basis. Kids often won't share all these things if they have limited time with the other parent. It is up to you to keep the other parent informed. Purchase a dozen or so 9x12 envelopes and a book of stamps. Let your child write the parent's address on the envelope (young children will enjoy decorating these with stickers or crayons). Then have her place items from school or home in the envelope and mail one envelope a week. It may help to keep a pad of sticky-notes near the envelopes for writing quick messages. This gives your child a way to feel connected with the other parent throughout the week.

> If it is feasible, let your child have an extended stay (one month or more) with the other parent so that they know it is not just "fun with the other parent," and so you can take time for yourself and re-evaluate your goals and priorities.
> *Lori Wilson*
> *Redlands, California*

Say thanks. Even if the kids are a little late getting home, or didn't take a full nap...say thank you.

NOTES FOR THE NON-CUSTODIAL PARENT

There may be a sense of relief when leaving a bad relationship. That sense of relief can quickly be replaced by guilt, frustration or anger as you try to understand your role in your child's life.

Your role as a mother or father remains the same. You still need to provide the same guidance and love. The only difference is that you won't be doing it in-person each day. Don't underestimate your importance to your children. Though you are not living with them day to day, they need you as much as always.

> Write letters to your kids and ask them to write letters to you as Birthday or Father's Day gifts. Letter writing got me through many Sunday evenings after I did a great job as a single parent all weekend and then had to "switch back" to bachelorhood.
> *Jim Burke*
> *Ponder, Texas*

Here are some ideas for staying actively involved in your child's life:

- Set up a visitation schedule and keep it. Buy your child a pocket calendar and highlight the days she will spend with you. This way she can look at the calendar and know when she will see you next.

- Encourage your child to bring homework or school projects with her on visits. This will keep you up to date on what your child is learning and allow you to help her study or do research.

- Have a set of "necessities" at your house for your child. Have a toothbrush, favorite stuffed animal, socks, extra clothing, etc. This will make your house feel more like the home that it should, versus a place the child is "visiting."

- If you have more than one child, schedule some one-on-one time with each child during your time together.

- Stay positive. Picking up and delivering your children may be a difficult task. The custodial parent may always have a few words of wisdom for you. Be polite and listen, but don't let anyone take away from the relationship that you are maintaining with your children.

LONG DISTANCE PARENTING

Long distance parenting can work successfully with a little effort from both parents. Here are some ideas to try…

- Purchase large envelopes and write little notes to your child each day or every other day. Pick up little treasures for your child. These need not be expensive items, just little things to let your child know about your location.

- Take photographs monthly. Your child will be more comfortable having a visual image of where you are.

- Provide your child with envelopes with your address and postage. He can collect school papers, projects and notes to send your way.

- Consider installing an 800 number or providing your child with a cordless phone and phone card. This way your child can call you at any time without having to explain to anyone who he is calling or why.

- Budget for visits. No matter what the reason for the distance, it is the parents' responsibility to make sure enough money is allotted for plane, bus or train fares.

- For younger children, tape record a new bedtime story once a week.

- If your child has a computer, consider getting on-line and communicating through e-mail and chat rooms. This can be a lot less costly than phone calls, while also providing a way to send letters instantly.

> Always talk evenly about the other parent, remembering this child loves that person very much—no matter what.
> *Deborah Critzerr*
> *Ventura, California*

- Find out what your child is studying in school. Try to find items that he may want to share with his class or incorporate in a school project.

- With a young child, start a round robin story or letter. You write ½ of a page and then send it to your child. She writes ½ a page and sends it back to you. Continue this rotation until the story is completed. This can help younger children feel comfortable writing.

JOINT CUSTODY

Joint custody seems to work best with older children who can handle moving between homes. Younger children need a sense of security which can be hard to create in a joint custody arrangement—but

> Try to let children have a "desensitize" time when they get home from being with the other parent. Don't make big plans for a couple of hours. This helps offer them an adjustment period.
> *Karen Minot*
> *Lakewood, Colorado*

possible if the parents work well together. The starting point for maximizing the positives in a joint custody arrangement begins with open communication between parents.

- Decide on house rules. Keep house rules as consistent as possible between homes.

- Decide on allowance.

- Get out your calendars and sort through extracurricular activities. If your child signs up for swimming, can you work his pick-up and drop-off times into your schedules?

- Go through your child's events day by day. Try to sort out any rules or scheduling conflicts that might arise in advance.

- Focus on a pick up/drop off ritual. What time can you expect one another? (It is a good idea to give the kids a little warning, too. Let them know 30-45 minutes beforehand to get ready to go to Mom or Dad's house.)

• Know that if a child seems distant towards the end of a visit he is probably preparing for the transition to go to the other parent's home.

> Parents focus too much on revenge and use child support and visitation as tools. It is time to stop the revenge and stop hurting children.
> *Single Mother*
> *Orlando, Florida*

• Meet regularly. Be open to meeting each month and discussing how the kids are doing. Do this in a businesslike manner when the children are not present. If you sense problems or difficulties with the arrangement or a difference in household rules, bring them up! Trying to keep the differences inside, will only cause an uproar later.

THE PITFALLS OF CUSTODY:
GAMES PARENTS PLAY
THAT YOU'LL WANT TO AVOID

Whether it be out of hurt, anger or insecurity, parents and children all too often succumb to mind-games and other games that can only lead to hurt, misunderstandings and frustration.

As part of successful single-parenting, it's important to vow not to engage in these games. If you are working with another parent who is not mature enough to make the same vow, keep your end of the deal, anyway. Children deserve respect and respectful parents. Eventually, they will thank you for it.

Spoil Sport - Longing to make up for lost time or sway a child's love or appreciation, a parent may be tempted to overindulge a child in gifts. This is most commonly seen with non-custodial parents who irregularly spend time

> When dealing with custody issues, remember to put what is in the best interest of your child ahead of your best interests.
> *L.D.*
> *Morehead City, North Carolina*

with their children. If this describes you, realize that your child wants your love, not your gifts. Teaching your child that money or gifts is equivalent to love is not an inspiring model.

Child Spies - Never ask a child to "find out" information for you or pry about her time spent with the other parent. As an adult, if you have a question, ask the other adult. Children deserve to be kids.

Children as Pawns - Unless there are viable concerns for a child's well-being, there is no reason to withhold visitation. I have seen parents who withhold visitation for child support, anger or bitterness. While this does work to hurt the other parent, you are hurting the child, too. That's not fair. Parents who don't remedy this will have to account to their children when they start asking questions later. And believe me, they will.

Brainwashing - Never try to sway a child's view or opinion of another parent. Offer only factual information. Your child has a right to form his own opinion of each parent. Parents who brainwash their children will have to account to these children as they get older. Most likely, a time will come when children will seek out the other parent, and learn that much of what was said was not factually accurate. This sort of behavior has destroyed many once solid child-parent relationships. Don't let it happen to you.

DEALING WITH AN ABSENT PARENT

Sixty-nine percent of our survey participants sought ways to explain and handle the absence of the other parent in their child's life. While each situation requires unique consideration, there are some basics that are applicable to all relationships.

Tell it like it is. Do not sugarcoat reality. If the parent is not there because the parent chose not to be, or has an addiction that prevents involvement, or has other extenuating limitations, do not gloss these over "for the child's sake." A well-meant lie will eventually require more lies to maintain. With only one parent for your child to lean on, it's important that the feelings of trust between you and your child are solid.

On the other hand, make sure what you tell your child is factual. You may have your own negative feelings about the child's other parent, but try not to let these feelings slip into your statements about the parent's absence.

Find a role model. Finding a role model is always important when a parent is absent. Children grow in a more balanced way when they are exposed to both male and female role models. These role models do not need to be parents. If an adult male is absent from your home, seek a family friend, counselor, pastor or a Big Brother program so your child has a role model to talk to. Likewise, if an adult female is absent from the home, seek a surrogate model for your child. A good role model who will spend time with your child on a regular basis will also take some pressure off your shoulders. You'll know that person can help teach your child values, morals and offer counsel during times of turmoil. Try to choose a role model whose values match your own and will be there for your child for years to come.

Handling a child's anger. As the only parent around, you will have the rewards of seeing all your child's successes. With this, however, often comes the downside of receiving your child's anger. When a parent is absent, the child often can only lash out at the present parent. This displaced anger is common and it's important for you to recognize it for what it is. Don't meet this anger with your own anger or rebuttal. Let your child vent. And later, offer discussion and a forum for your child to express his feelings. Also, work on healthy outlets to relieve anger and emotions.

> Work as hard as possible to keep from being negative about the other parent. It's just too tough on the kids to hear that, and it causes problems that it may take years to work through.
>
> *Single Mother*
> *Helena, Montana*

Improving self-worth. In Chapter Eleven, we talk about how children of different age groups respond to the single-parent transition. When a parent is already absent, this response is often more intense, and children often won't want to discuss it. Young children who don't understand the dynamics of this family form, may blame themselves for a parent's absence. Much reassurance is needed for a child to overcome this fear. Remember that your child may question her self-worth because of this. Each time this questioning occurs, you can offer a positive affirmation to your child about how important she is to you and to your family.

The fear of abandonment. A child in a single-parent home often fears abandonment. This fear increases when one parent is rarely, if ever, around. Stability, reassurance and patience can help ease a child's fear. If you think your child is having a hard time with the fear of abandonment, talk to a trusted counselor or psychotherapist.

The fear of intimacy. Many things can contribute to a fear of intimacy. When a child sees their mother or father hurt physically or emotionally, fear of intimacy may arise. A child's understanding of boundaries will also blur. Introducing your child to healthy relationships of your own can help a child to deal with this fear.

With the fear of intimacy and the fear of abandonment come many signs. A child who fears abandonment may be very controlling or needy. A child who fears intimacy may develop a close friendship or relationship, only to retreat later. As your child moves through adolescent friendships, and early adult relationships, watch to see if these fears surface. Consider seeking the help of a professional if you see your child suffering from these fears.

Healthy relationship role models. My parents divorced when I was eight months old, and my mother never chose to remarry. I was not exposed to many healthy role models of adult relationships. Because of this, I was confused about healthy boundaries and what to expect from a partner. As a child, I learned about relationships from books, television and what I heard from my peers. As one might imagine, this didn't give me a realistic outlook. After failing

> Don't poison your child's mind against the other parent—even though at times, you might like to!
> *Dale Winchell*
> *Cherry Hill, New Jersey*

at friendships and relationships throughout childhood and early adulthood, I was fortunate enough to find a good psychotherapist to help me understand healthy intimate relationships.

As a single parent, you can help your child by exposing her to other healthy couples that you know. Try spending time

> Do what you need to do to forget your feelings towards the other parent. Try to accept that person's decision to be or not be a part of the child's life. Let their relationship be separate from your own.
> *M.B.*
> *Dallas, Texas*

with other couples who have a solid and respectful relationship. If you don't know anyone like this, or are new to a community, talk to your child about relationships, friendships, intimacy, trust and respect. Be on the lookout for unrealistic notions from the media, television and books.

Kids' Speak:
What I Wish My Parents Knew
About Life In A Single Parent Family

Have you ever wished you could get inside the mind of your child? Have you had problems with communication and yearned to understand his or her thinking? Youth across the country desire to have their opinions known. Yet, out of fear, embarrassment, or lack of opportunity their thoughts go unheard. Here youth take the spotlight, speaking openly and honestly about the concerns of today's children.

What would you like the parent you live with to know?

"Most of all, I hope my Dad knows how much I appreciate him. I know raising kids on your own can't be easy. I don't say as often as I could how much I love him, but he means the world to me, as a role model, dad and buddy."

-David, Age 17

"Sometimes I feel guilty for visiting my Dad. I come home and my Mom wants to know everything. If he buys me something she'll say,

'Oh like that makes up for him not being there for four years. I know they had their problems and don't get along, but I don't think that should mean that I can't like my Dad."

-Jennifer, Age 13

"Ever since my Dad left, my Mom has a lot less time. When the weekend comes she makes a big production out of making sure we go somewhere and do something really special. We go to an amusement park or shopping. At first it was fun, but now I would rather just have twenty minutes a day where we could just hang out and talk."

-Todd, Age 15

Your child has enough love for both parents. There is no reason to try to "buy" their love, or become a pushover because your child gets upset and cries for the other parent. Parenting is not a competition. Be yourself!

J. Latham
West Des Moines, Iowa

"My Mom will cry and it makes me sad."

-Elsa, Age 4

"I don't like it when they fight about money. I hear them on the phone, and it makes me feel like I just want to get away."

-Tony, Age 10

"She needs to get a life. She always wants to talk to me, go out for dinner, do shopping together and talk to my friends. It is like I'm my Dad. I was going to send in one of those personal letters like in 'Sleepless in Seattle!' She needs to go out and meet people because what happens when I move out? I don't plan on living here forever."

-Sam, Age 16

"I don't think she realizes that she uses the divorce as an excuse for everything. I'll ask if we can go to the zoo and she'll say 'We don't have money, we could have if your dad hadn't left.' Somebody will ask her to do something and she'll say 'I can't I am going through a divorce.' I don't use it as an excuse, why should she?"

-Jane, Age 12

"My Mom always wants to talk to me about the divorce and how it makes me feel. I don't want to talk about it, maybe later when I'm ready."

-Frederick, Age 8

"She is a good Mom, she does a good job. I wish she would do a little more for herself instead of always focusing on us. I told her that once, and she just laughed. I guess she didn't think I was serious."

-Rick, Age 13

"He doesn't have to be SUPERDAD. He goes to work and then comes home, does laundry, cooks, he wants to do everything. I try to help and he'll say 'Oh no, I can get that' I wish he knew it is okay to ask for help, I mean, we are a family."

-Cynthia, Age 13

What would you like the parent you don't live with to know?
"When I visit my Dad, he has his friends over and stuff. I think that time should be just for me. There is so much I need to tell him, and I don't get the chance."

-Charles, Age 14

"I miss her. I wish she would want to see me."

-Julia, Age 7

"We will stay close throughout this. A divorce can't separate us. He will always be as important to me as he was when he lived at home. Nothing anyone can say will ever change that."

-Kent, Age 17

"I know he tried everything he could to make the marriage work. I respect him and I miss him so much."
-Danielle, Age 12

"My Dad seems to think since he lives across the country he doesn't need to visit us regularly. It's not right, we are still his kids. If he wanted to move that far away, then he should have the money to fly us there. If you ask me, he is running away from it all. But then he will call once a month and want to be all lovey. And I'm like, "Who is this?"
-Rose, Age 16

"On the weekends I spend with my Mom, she always buys me a ton of stuff. Those things aren't important to me, only she is."
-Jeanette, Age 14

"I wish he knew that I want to spend time with him. When we visit he spends all his time with my brother, and that's not fair. They always got along better than we did when we all lived together, but I still need him to."
-Karen, Age 15

"Our time together should be spent catching up, not talking about Mom."
-Troy, Age 11

I don't like it when he always has friends over when we are with him. I think the weekend should be our time."
-Lania, 12

"I love him."
-Elsa, Age 4

RESOURCES FOR CUSTODY

Handbook on Child Support Enforcement is a free, 50 page, how-to guide for getting the payments owed to you and your children. This brochure lists state and federal offices. Request brochure 638D from the Consumer Information Center, Pueblo, CO 81009.

National Coalition for Child Support Reform "was created to investigate child support laws, as well as discover what attorneys, enforcement office workers, and custodial/non-custodial parents perceive to be the problems and concerns with current enforcement systems. We are also interested in what is right with the system and what tools and procedures are working well. With this knowledge, the NCCSR hopes to devise a reform plan to bring about positive change." You can aid this organization by completing a brief survey. You can find the survey online at *http://home.navisoft.com/solemom/nccsr.htm*

Federal Office of Child Support Home Page is a good source for information. Their web site features news, reports, policy documents and links to state program web sites. Check it out at *http://www.acf.dhhs.gov/programs/CSE/index.html*

Child Support Network "locates missing parents and collects and enforces court ordered child support payments." They offer several payment plans, including a no collection, no fee plan. For more information call (800) 398-0700 or write to: Child Support Network, 1528 E. Missouri Avenue, Suite B-106, Phoenix, AZ 85014.

Single & Custodial Father's Network is a virtual organization with their worldwide membership being linked through resources on the World Wide Web. SCFN "is a member supported organization, dedicated to helping fathers to meet the challenge of being custodial parents. SCFN seeks to provide informational and supportive resources to custodial fathers and their families. SCFN's mission is to support single and custodial fatherhood through research, publications and interactive communications." Visit their web site at *http://www.single-fathers.org/* Or write to: Single and Custodial Fathers Network 1700 E. Carson Street, Pittsburgh, PA 15203.

Non Custodial Parents Resource Center is a nonprofit organization assisting non-custodial parents to maintain their rights to be with their children. This grass roots, civil rights organization is dedicated to the parents and children who do not have access or custody to each other because of divorce. The mission of NCPRC "is to provide the Non-Custodial Parent and the Practicing Professional with a one stop source for educational resources that they need in order to strengthen their goals of maintaining their rights as parents and providers." Visit their web site at *http://WWW.Bayou.com/~ncfc*

Alliance for Non-Custodial Parents Rights "is a nonprofit corporation dedicated to protecting and promoting the civil and inalienable rights of non-custodial parents and their families." The active organization offers chances for members to join in urgent action and calls for change in the current law. For information visit their web site at *http://www.ancpr.org/ancprindex.html* or write to: ANCPR, 9903 Santa Monica Blvd., Suite 207, Beverly Hills, CA 90212.

The Child Support Report is a newsletter published monthly by the National Office of Child Support Enforcement. To be added to the mailing list write to: *Child Support Report*, Office of Child Support Enforcement, 370 L'Enfants Promenade SW, 4th Floor, Washington, DC 20447.

CHAPTER TEN
FINDING
QUALITY CHILD CARE

With child care expenses averaging as the third highest household expense, it makes sense to give this area thorough research, time and evaluation. The right child care provider can also offer tremendous peace of mind.

Fortunately, more and more child care options are becoming available, and more and more organizations exist to help us sort through the options.

WHAT TYPE OF CARE ARE YOU LOOKING FOR?

There are four basic types of care.

Family Care Provider - These caregivers provide care for children in their home (and often have children themselves) as their career. The quality of these caregivers is diverse. Some are certified, participate in healthy food programs and provide a structured environment. Others may want to deal only in cash or spend too much time running their home instead of taking care of children.

I, personally, have had great experiences with family child care providers for my daughter. I have worked with two different caregivers since Samantha was born and loved them both. The hours and benefits have been great and the amount of one-on-one attention has helped my daughter excel in confidence and preschool skills. But there are drawbacks to family child care. If the caregiver is sick, or if one of her own children is sick, there is typically no care for the day. Caregivers may have regular vacation time for which an alternate arrangement is not provided. There is also no guarantee that the caregiver will remain in business, and hours may not be as flexible allowing early drop off and late pick ups. (Though in my experience, the hours have been equally, if not more, flexible.)

On the plus side, the rates can be less expensive than traditional or in-home care. This option also provides interaction with other children but doesn't have as many children on the premises as a day care facility. This results in less sick days and more personalized attention.

DAY CARE

This is the most common form of child care, the traditional day care center. Some are franchised and others are privately owned. These institutions offer structured environments and caregivers who usually need to be trained in several areas. The hours are often flexible, and you'll have little need for a back up service.

As for drawbacks, it's one of the more expensive options. Also there are more children present which means more germs and more sick days. Make sure to check rules and health codes to see how well they minimize the potential spread of germs.

Also ask about the turnover rate of the caregivers. It's hard on children to become attached to one caregiver only for her to leave and a replacement to follow suit.

IN-HOME PROVIDERS

On the plus side, an in-home provider eliminates the morning crunch of waking up a whole household to get children to their destinations. Likewise, you avoid the race of picking up children from an outside provider after work. There is also the added comfort of knowing that your children will be in a familiar environment.

The primary disadvantage is lack of interaction with other children. If you choose this outlet, make sure to provide some play time with other children.

COMMUNITY CHILD CARE

For those working part time or within a very limited budget, a community sponsored child care can provide a great opportunity. Many times churches, schools and other organizations provide morning care for children for a low fee. The drawbacks are that the hours are usually quite limited, and it's often more of a free play environment than a structured learning environment. Check with your local town or city center to see if these opportunities exist in your neighborhood.

A spin-off on community-based care is to pool resources with other single parents and hire a full-time caregiver to watch several children in the home of a parent who works full time.

LIVE-IN CARE

A nanny or AuPair is yet another option to consider for child raising. These caretakers provide the greatest flexibility. The disadvantages of this option include lack of privacy and often less training than some of the other options.

PREPARING FOR THE SEARCH

Begin by browsing through your yellow pages and jotting down local providers. Ask friends who they currently use and who have they have used. Contact your local Child Care Resource and Referral Agency (CCR&R) for more ideas on contacts (see resources). And don't forget your local paper as a source. I found both my providers through the paper.

Once you have compiled a list of names to work from, it's time to get organized. Keeping detailed records of your search will help you save time and make the best-informed decision. I recommend developing a screening sheet for each stage. For phone interviews, have a list of questions you will ask each caregiver and leave space to jot in their answers. Call every care provider on your list before advancing to the in-person interview stage.

After you have completed collecting information via phone, choose the providers that best match your needs. Plan on visiting these caregivers for an in-person interview. Also, be sure to check references using a worksheet, like the one provided later in this chapter.

Sample Phone Screening Sheet

(As you make your own sheet, you may want to copy the following items in order of their importance to you for easier reference.)

Name_____Phone_____

Contact Person_____

Type of Care_____

What are the hours?_____

What are the rates?_____

What meals and snacks are included?_____

Is a nutritional program followed?_____

What are their requirements of children's health? (i.e. when is a child sent home as "sick?")_____

What requirements must the caregivers meet?_____

What is the structure of a typical day?_____

What sterilization procedures are followed with regards to toys, changing areas, etc.?_____

If your child is nearing toilet training age, what type of assistance is offered?_____

How is discipline handled?_____

Where do children sleep? Is the area safe and monitored appropriately?_____

Are field trips and outings offered? If yes, will you receive a permission slip in advance to sign and return?_____

Is there a trial period before a firm commitment is made?_____

Should you need to end or switch child care, what notice, if any, is required?_____

How long has the operation been in business?_____

Are surprise visits allowed or encouraged?_____

Can you stop in and take your child out to lunch?_____

Are the play areas secure from outsiders?_____

What is the caregiver to child ratio?_____

Additional Questions About Day Care Centers

What is the turnover rate amongst caregivers?_____

For older children, do they provide drop-off and pick-up service from school? _____

Did the person who answered the phone seem friendly, informative and knowledgeable? _____

Did the provider encourage that you stop in any time or offer a range of times?_____

Additional Questions For Family and Group Providers

Are you guaranteeing to pay a certain amount per week? Some in-home providers require the fee be paid whether your child is there or not. Also check to see what you are obligated to pay during vacation times. _____

Do they make sure all children are current on immunizations and require a signed record from the doctor? _____

When taking on new children, does the service allow for a trial period in case the child does not fit into the routine?_____

Why did they choose to start a family care business?_____

What training and certification do they have? _____

Do they know CPR and is their certification current? Do they have first-aid training? _____

Is there any smoking within the environment? _____

Will anyone besides the caregiver be present? If so, who?_____

Does the provider have a backup caregiver in the event she is sick or her own children get sick?_____

Will you be provided with monthly or weekly receipts? _____

If something comes up at work at the last minute, could the caregiver cover for an extra hour if needed?_____

Does the caregiver have a car available to get children to the doctor in the case of an emergency?_____

What age group of children does she care for? Will your child have playmates close to her age?_____

How many kids are there now? Does she have intentions of bringing on any more? _____

How long does she plan on staying in the business? _____

Additional Questions For In-Home Caregivers (all but question four are also appropriate for Live-In Caregivers.)

What do you enjoy most about your job? _____

What are your best qualities for this line of work? _____

Do you plan on staying at this place of employment for the next few years?_____

Do you have any of your own children? If so, where do they go for care? _____

How would you handle a child who wanted a toy that he was not allowed to have? (or other hypothetical question that might relate to your child. i.e., How would you handle a child that was adamant about not wanting to nap?) _____

What type of training and certification do you have?_____

How long have you been doing this work and what is your average length of employment with a household?_____

THE IN-PERSON VISIT

Watch, look and listen when you go for your in-person visit. I recommend visiting alone at first. Once you have narrowed your list down to two or three final choices, take your child along and watch her reaction.

I can't overstate the importance of taking your child with you to the potential center before making a commitment. When I engaged in child care search, I visited one very established child care center. I thought it was beautiful and provided worlds of opportunity for my daughter. Even though it was a bit more than I wanted to spend, I was hooked. Luckily, I decided to go back one more time with my daughter for an hour long observation. While there, she showed me things that I would have missed. I stood in the background and watched her interaction. She was scolded for taking a toy, even though no one had explained the rules. When we all went outside for play time, in less than five minutes she had walked to the area for the children ages nine and over. She was far enough out of vision that something could have easily happened to her. Additionally, she was climbing on playground equipment much above her skill level. Based on these factors, I continued my search.

Here is a sheet to use when evaluating in person:

Are the toys age-appropriate? _____

What is on the walls? Are there different types of artwork? Pictures of the alphabet? _____

Do they provide an information sheet each day listing the activities done, any items needed, etc.? _____

How are the children? Do they seem happy and well-behaved? Do they seem to listen and respect the teachers? _____

Is the outside area safe with only age-appropriate toys and clear barriers between different age groups? _____

Does the caregiver get down on the child's level? Do they listen intently? _____

Is the area clean and sanitized? _____

For Family Care Providers

Where are the toys kept? Is the area where children spend most of their time away from the television and other adult distractions?_____

_____

How safe is the home? Are stairways gated for young children? If they watch young and older children, are the older children's toys kept out of reach of the younger kids?_____

What is the outside like? Is there an outside play area? Is it safe from any busy traffic areas? Is the equipment age-appropriate? _____

For In Home Providers

(These visits often occur in your own home. Watch for the following.)

Does the potential caregiver ask questions about your children?_____

Does the caregiver inquire about photos, children's artwork, etc.? ____

If children are present how does the caregiver introduce themselves?

_____

What is the child's initial reaction to the caregiver?_____

CHECKING REFERENCES

After conducting extensive interviews by phone and in-person, you may be leaning toward a couple of providers as strong favorites. Before signing up though, it is important to check references. Ask any place that you are considering for at least three contacts. If a day care center will not release parents' names, ask to leave your name and number and for parents to contact you. Checking references at a day-care center isn't that common, but for peace of mind I think it is important.

What to ask referrals:

How long did they use the provider? _____

How did they hear of the provider? (This informs you if this is some-one who is a friend or relative, or a person who is completely objective.)_____

How old was their child when in this care?_____

Why did they cease to use the provider?_____

How often did the child get sick?_____

What was their favorite and least favorite part of the service? _____

How would they describe the caregiver?_____

Did they find the hours convenient and the service flexible?_____

Would they use this person (organization) again?_____

After following the above process you should feel confident that you are making the most informed and best choice possible for you and your child.

Keep all of your research in a folder for future reference. As your lifestyle changes and your child ages, you may want to change providers. This information will be both valuable and timesaving. It can also be a great resource for friends or co-workers who are looking for child care.

DEVELOPING A GOOD WORKING RELATIONSHIP

Communication is the key to any good relationship including the one you have with your child care provider. Interestingly though, communication about our children can be difficult for many parents. We often take any criticism of our child to be a personal criticism or we rise to their defense. Work on listening to your provider and giving feedback instead of reacting defensively.

In order to enhance your child care program, try the following ideas:

- Try to arrive ten minutes early in the morning or evening to talk to the provider about your child's day.

- When possible offer something to enhance the learning process. If children are studying the alphabet, and you have a great video, offer to loan it to them.

- For young children especially, keep consistency in discipline. Talk to your provider and agree on how to handle rules and outbursts. This will make care easier around the clock—otherwise children have one set of rules for child care hours and a separate set of rules for time spent with Mom or Dad. This complicates discipline roles for both parties.

- Monthly or bimonthly, try to meet with your provider for 20-30 minutes either in person or via phone Discuss your child's progress. Find out how she relates with other kids. Learn which activities she especially enjoys or excels in. Discuss any problem areas and brainstorm ideas for improvement.

- Develop an action plan for any crises that develop. Provide your caregiver with a complete emergency phone list including your child's doctor and clinic, your home, work, cellular and pager numbers. Include an alternate contact should you be unavailable. Update the list as needed.

SURVIVING THE FIRST WEEK

The first week of day care is the most difficult. Often, it's more difficult for the parent than the child. I'll admit, as will many of my friends, that I suffer from an overactive imagination. When I took my nine month-old daughter to her first family care provider, I dropped her off and gave her a huge hug and kiss. I handed Lisa a million pages of numbers and instructions. Then I left—with the diaper bag. After driving two miles I turned around and returned the diaper bag.

As I left (for the second time) my overactive imagination kicked in full force. I had visions of Lisa—not really being Lisa. I was convinced that she had just bought this house in a gorgeous subdivision and was using fake furniture to pose as a caregiver. And when I returned, both Lisa and my daughter would be gone. The previous night I had been full of confidence. But on drop-off day I was a wreck, despite checking three references. Imagine my surprise when I returned to find both Lisa and Samantha happily sitting on the couch cooing to each other. Day one was survived.

Tips for surviving the first couple weeks of day care:

Ease into it. If possible start with half days or three hours of attendance to let children ease into the environment and get into the groove. (And it allows you time to do the same!)

Realize it will take time. Plan on giving both you and your child a month to get accustomed to the new routine and arrangement.

Don't dawdle. It's important to give your child a hug and kiss good bye versus sneaking out, but be careful not to dawdle. Say your good-byes—and then go—don't draw it out.

Have a little faith - Don't dwell on guilt or worry. If you have followed the process in this chapter, you have done everything you can to ensure a positive and nurturing environment for your child. Give yourself a break, and a pat on the back. You've earned it.

A ONE MONTH CHECK UP: TO BE OR NOT TO BE?

Signs that your child care arrangement is working:

- Your child is eager and excited when you bring up going to child care.
- Your child is bringing home projects on a regular basis.
- You notice an improvement in a child's listening and/or verbal skills.
- Your child talks about activities that he or she did.
- Your child talks positively about other children at the program.

Signs that it may not be working:

- Your child seems leery of the child care center or unusually shy after a proper adjustment period has passed.
- Your child is frequently suffering from colds or flu.
- Your child is not bringing projects home or showing advancement of skills.
- Drop in visits are discouraged.
- There is a change in your child's eating or sleeping pattern.
- A child stays close to you at drop off time instead of joining in with other kids.

If you have concerns about your child's behavior or attitude toward child care, talk to your provider. If the situation cannot be remedied, return to your search.

RESOURCES FOR FINDING QUALITY CHILD CARE

BOOKS

The *Dear Baby Sitter Handbook* by Vicki Lansky contains everything your baby sitter might need to know! "From vital phone numbers on the opening page, to a caretaker medical release form, play ideas, bedtime tips, first aid info and more." This 60 page book is available for $4.95. Order at your local bookstore or order direct from Practical Parenting, 15245 Minnetonka, Blvd., Minnetonka, MN 55345-1510.

CHILD CARE RESOURCE AND REFERRAL AGENCIES

Child Care Resource and Referral Agencies (CCR&R) play an important part in assessing options available to you. These nonprofit organizations exist to inform parents of the local options available to families. When contacting a CCR&R it's good to have some basic ideas formulated on the type of care you are looking for and a brief description of your child's personality. Check your phone book to see if there is a CCR&R listed. If not, call Child Care Aware at 800-424-2246 and ask for the closest contact.

Child Care Aware is an organization devoted to ensuring that every parent has access to good information about finding quality child care and resources in their community. Send a SASE to receive the brochure *Give Your Child Something That Will Last A Lifetime...* This brochure details how to find good quality child care and things you should look for in a provider. Write to: Child Care Aware, 2116 Campus Drive SE, Rochester, MN 55904.

Nonprofit Association of Those in the In-home Child Care Industry "is an educational association for nannies and those who educate, place, employ and support professional in-home child care providers."

A free information packet is available by writing to International Nanny Association, 900 Haddon Avenue, Suite 438, Collingswood, NJ 08108. Or call (800) 297-1477. You can also visit their web site at *www.nanny.org* For parents considering a nanny, request the brochure *A Nanny for Your Family: Answers to questions parents often ask about in-home child care.*

FAMILY CHILD CARE PROVIDERS

The NAFCC offers information on home-based child-care issues and publishes the *National Directory of Family Child Care Associations and Support Groups* and provides referrals to local family child care providers that are accredited. Contact: NAFCC, 725 15th St. NW, Suite 505, Washington, DC 20005. Or call (202) 347-3300.

ONLINE INFORMATION

The Child Care Experts National Network was developed to help parents and employers access information about child development, child care, early education, family support and dependent care resources from local experts across the country. For information, visit their web site at *http://www.childcare-experts.org/*

RUNNING A CHILD CARE BUSINESS

For information on starting your own child care business contact: The National Association for Family Child Care, 1331 A Pennsylvania Ave., NW Suite 348, Washington, DC 20004.

TAX BRIEFS

A credit for a portion of your child care expenses can be obtained by using the Child and Dependent Care Tax Credit. (CDCTC). Regardless of income level, the Credit can reduce your federal, and in some cases state, income taxes.

Earned Income Credit (IEC) provides a refund for some low-income families—even if you don't owe taxes. For questions call the National Women's Law Center at (202) 328-5160 or the Center on Budget and Policy Priorities at (202) 408-1080.

Check with your employer to see if a pretax cafeteria plan is available for your child care.

If you use an in-home caregiver or live-in caregiver you may be responsible for paying Social Security tax. Contact your local IRS office for form 942. You will also need an employment identification number. Contact your accountant or local IRS office for more information on the tax implications of using an in-home care provider. IRS Publications 15 (Circular E) and 503 are good places to start.

CHAPTER ELEVEN
IMPROVING CHILDREN'S EMOTIONAL HEALTH

As you can probably imagine, it was impossible to find a parent in our survey who wasn't concerned with some aspect of her child's emotions. Some parents yearned for better communication, others wanted to understand how children felt about the single-parent family form, and still others wanted to learn practical ways to raise healthy, responsible and resilient children.

This chapter will explore many of the complex issues that face today's children within the single-parent family. The resource section also contains a compre-

> Help your child stay involved in school, community and church activities. My child has lost many of his old friends during the divorce. I think that these children didn't know what to say to him, so they avoided him. This resulted in his feeling alienated, alone, different. Encouraging his involvement in normal activities has helped him to feel connected to his peers and community.
>
> *Single Mother*
> *Denver, Colorado*

hensive listing of contacts for information about tough issues facing today's children.

AGES AND STAGES

Children of different age groups will be impacted differently by the single-parent family form. This section outlines some of the ways children are affected. In order to cover the material, we must generalize a bit about the most common affects on specific age groups. Please remember, though, that not all children will be affected the same way. Likewise, an adjustment period might vary by weeks, months or years from one child to another. Use the summaries below as guidelines. When in doubt, contact a mental health professional or one of the resources at the end of this chapter.

Some of the information may be more noticeable when a child first enters into the single-parent family form. Locate your child's age in the summaries below and also read the summary for one age group younger and one age group older, since it's common for children's reactions to overlap.

THE SINGLE-PARENT FAMILY TRANSITION PERIOD: HOW IT AFFECTS YOUR CHILD

> At bedtime we talk about the *Worst Thing That Happened To Me Today* followed by *The Best Thing That Happened To Me Today.* You can learn a lot about your child and yourself this way.
>
> *Single Mother*
> *Vancouver, Washington*

INFANTS

An infant will detect any changes in her needs being met. If two parents actively provided food, comfort and other necessities for the child, she will notice the different motions and the absence of a parent.

Infants can sense a parent's distress or upset. Try to maintain a calmness around your infant. If times are particularly trying, ask a calm and confident friend to help out.

TODDLERS & PRESCHOOLERS

A preschooler will often feel confused during the single-parent family transition. Accustomed to routines and schedules, a young child is often impacted by physical and emotional changes and challenges. Maintaining regular schedules and discipline will help preschoolers maintain a sense of stability.

A young child may also feel helpless. While she might yearn to control or change the situation, she does not have the means to do so. In an attempt to control the situation, a child may turn unknowingly to emotional manipulation to control one or both parents. Stay alert for these behavior patterns in your child. If you feel your child is angrier or whining more often than normal, keep your discipline in place and encourage other outlets to help your child talk and release her emotions. If the child has a younger sibling, keep close watch that she doesn't vent her anger onto him.

At this age, a child's questions and concerns are fairly self-centered. The absence of a parent might mean, "Who will bathe me and blow bubbles in the tub?" or other questions that are equally self-focused. Reassure your child that all of his needs will continue to be met.

One important distinction between a toddler and a child of preschool age, is the level of understanding. In just a couple of years, from ages two to four, the level of understanding and knowledge gained is incredible. While toddlers won't understand the single-parent family form, a preschooler will begin to grasp the concept. It is equally important to realize that preschoolers are prone

> Be involved and listen to what your children have to say. It might sound like dribble to you, but if it's important enough for a child to say it's important enough for you to listen. Keep the lines of communication open. One day it could be something extremely important, and a child needs to know he can come to you with anything.
>
> *K. Rhoden*
> *Houston, Texas*

to fill in what they don't understand with fantasies. Be attentive to your child's imaginings.

The preschooler has also completed the task of separating herself from the parent. This often leads to a fear of abandonment or self-blame and guilt. Fears of abandonment can recur throughout a lifetime if separation between parent and child occurs when a child is young. Parental involvement will help to minimize this fear. Solid answers, explanations and encouragement will also help.

> Write down what you wish to instill/provide for your children and what you can do daily to accomplish this (not forgetting what you need to do for yourself in order to do it with love and in good health and periodically read and update it.)
>
> *Single Mother*
> *Toledo, Ohio*

It is not uncommon for a young child to begin waking in the middle of the night, have bad dreams, throw more temper tantrums or start to wet his pants. These are ways for a child to release his emotions—and in most cases, the behavior should be discussed instead of punished.

If a parent is absent during this time, a toddler or preschooler may rely heavily on, and cling to, the parent that is present. Watch for this behavior and reassure your child so not to create an unhealthy dependency.

EARLY ELEMENTARY (GRADES 1-4)

Imagination is at its peak in children of this age group. When left with unanswered questions or attempting to deny a situation, these children are quick to fabricate their own reality. Parents can help children by being as clear as possible about why the transition to a single-parent family occurred. This age group will have an easier time with the transition if regular contact is kept by the non-custodial parent and children see the new environment of the non-custodial parent.

Schoolwork may also be affected or a child may suffer lack of concentration. With a child's limited means of dealing with such strong emotions, it's important to watch for these situations. Should they occur, maintain solid communication with both your child and his teacher to help deal with, and overcome, the hardship.

THE PRETEEN YEARS (GRADES 5-8)

Children in this age group are concerned with how they fit in at school and how they compare to their peers. A change in family form may lead to a temporary withdrawal in activities they once excelled in. Children may also be hesitant or unsure of how to explain the new family form to their peers.

> At least once a week, slow down and have fun with your kids. It doesn't have to be expensive—you don't even have to 'go' anywhere. Just relax and let yourself remember what all the effort is really about.
>
> *Susan Challender*
> *Des Moines, Iowa*

Maintaining active communication with your child's teacher can help you tune in to your child's school concerns and help your child to deal with them more effectively. A strong network of emotional support will also be needed. Children at this age are learning to adjust to school schedules, peers, their changing bodies and trying to begin to put their feet down firmly in this world. As parents, we need to offer a strong emotional network as a foundation on which to stand.

A child may also become rebellious during this age period. Parents often share stories of a child lashing out with words like, "I hate you!" Realize that your child does not hate you. The child hates the divorce or separation that has taken "his" parents apart. These are ways of your child venting his emotion. When you sense this anger, try to offer additional outlets as a release.

ADOLESCENCE

At the adolescent age, children have usually been exposed to the single-parent family form and will not have as many questions as those in the younger age groups. Though they understand the single-parent family form, it's important to realize that they are often no better equipped to interpret or adapt to it.

When teens have grown accustomed to their two-parent family form, a change will bring an array of emotions. One day a teenager may be full of support and the next day, you might be met with anger or an emotional outburst.

For single-mother headed households with a son present, the son may find himself filling the shoes of "the man of the house" even when there had been a very active father. Single mothers can help relieve this responsibility by not assigning too many responsibilities to their sons and not using them as a sounding board for concerns and problems. Likewise, daughters of single-father headed households may try to continue with duties once done by the mother. Strive for an equal distribution of duties and ensure that the roles of parents do not fall on the children.

Adolescence also brings a whirlwind of questions to any teenager, no matter what their family form. Teenagers are struggling to find their role in society, family and among their peers. Often rebellion can serve to help teens break away from their old identity and encourage the creation of a new identity.

> Always remember that you are the primary role model in your child's life and live your life knowing that. I feel that this has made me a better person and I strive to make my life and myself better. I learned to love myself because I knew that I wanted my child to grow up loving herself and if she didn't sense me loving myself she would never know how!
>
> *Melissa Thames*
> *Cincinnati, Ohio*

HELPING CHILDREN ADAPT

Many children reported a lost feeling during the transition months to a single-parent family form. With one or both parents often occupied with their own grief and concerns, children's needs are commonly overlooked. Anticipate that you will be unable to handle everything during these times. Set up a support system and alternate adult role models for your child to talk to. Often a role model who is not a relative is a great outlet for a child. This offers the child an opportunity to speak openly and honestly about one or both parents—without fear that she might anger or hurt a parent.

Parents can also help their children by keeping consistent rules, boundaries and discipline. In times of crises, there is a tendency to let rules and schedules slide. Stick as closely to rules as possible.

Allow children to have "off" days. In your own transition time to the single-parent family form, there will be days when you feel confident and sure of yourself, and other days where you are down and depleted. There isn't a word a person could mutter that would lift your spirits or put the bounce back in your step. Allow your child to have these same types of days. Be gentle as your child rides his emotional roller coaster and be as understanding as possible.

Answer questions truthfully. Children have not had the inside look at the reason for becoming a single-parent family form that you have. Even if a child has witnessed yelling or fighting, many more questions are bound to follow. Attempt to answer all questions truthfully, providing as much age-appropriate information as possible. Children are great detectives of falseness. And when a child doesn't believe you're telling him the truth, his imagination will create his own answer. These imaginings are almost always worse than the truth since in a child's thinking he will often hold himself responsible.

If divorce or separation is responsible for creating your single-parent family form, try to talk with the other parent about what the children will be told. Conflicting stories will only create difficult emotions and split loyalties among children.

Let your child know that all of his emotions are okay. There will be a complex set of emotions for any child throughout their growing up. Some of these emotions may be stronger when a child goes through a change, like the transition period to a single-parent family. It's especially important to not deny or invalidate your child's feelings—even when you are feeling overwhelmed by your own emotions. Let your child know that his anger, jealousy, sadness and other emotions are all healthy and normal. Talk about possible outlets for relieving pent-up emotions.

CHILDREN'S EMOTIONS

Many children are flooded with emotion after the divorce, loss or absence of a parent. The intensity of these emotions can frighten a child who has not felt them before. Children, just like adults, need support and time to work through their mixed emotions. As a parent, you can guide your child by learning about these emotions and their causes, and encouraging your child as he works through them.

Think of the range of emotions you felt when you separated, lost a spouse or had a child on your own. Your children will have many of the same feelings. Feelings of loss, anger and hurt are common and will often recur throughout the years. Children have one disadvantage. They don't understand many of these emotions. They don't know things will usually get better. They don't have the experience to deal with these problems. You can help your child through many of the emotional hurdles he will face. The first step is to understand your child's point of view. Here are what a few children had to say about the emotions they felt:

"The hardest part about losing my father was that I needed someone to talk to. My mom had her own problems to deal with. My friends were more into cars and things, so I never really talked it out. Now, my mom wants to talk, but I feel like everything is bottled up and I can't get it out." - *Jerry S.*

"I felt angry. Angry at my dad for not having the courage to make it work and angry at my mom for letting him go. Angry at myself that I couldn't see it. Angry at

> Make sure your kids can talk about their happy/sad and all other feelings about the divorce in a safe environment, even if you resent the other parent.
> *Deborah Critzer*
> *Ventura, California*

God for putting us through this. I turned to drinking and drugs because I didn't know how to get the anger out." - *Monica W.*

"Everything that was secure, wasn't anymore. I mean, I never thought this would happen in my family. " - *Kerri L.*

This is a sampling of emotions in children. Learning how, and taking the time, to identify your child's feelings can help prevent the emptiness many children feel. Let's examine each emotion more closely.

THE EMOTION: WORRY

When a child's environment is drastically changed, she will worry that more unwanted changes may come. Common worries of children include: worrying that something might happen to the absent parent, worrying they might be divorced from the family (this is more common in young children who do not understand divorce) or worrying that something might happen to the parent they live with and there will be no one to take care of them.

THE SIGNS

A child who worries a lot will ask questions for reassurance. "When will you be coming home?" The child may look for an exact time and begin to worry if you're even a few minutes late. Watch for questions that show a child is seeking constant reassurance such as, "You love me, right?" Or other questions that show the child is seeking affirmation of your feelings towards him.

IDEAS TO WORK WITH

You can ease a child's worries through reassurance and consistency. When you go out, let your child know when you will be home and be true to your word. This can minimize a child's fear that you won't return. The child may still ask each time you leave when you will be coming back and the process of eliminating that fear may take years.

Each time you come home on time, you are one step closer to abolishing that fear.

To minimize the fear that something might happen to the parent outside the home, let the child get to know that parent's environment. Many times, children don't

> Don't assume your children know that they are the most important part of your life, tell them this all the time.
> *Lori Wilson*
> *Redlands, California*

understand where that parent has gone, and introducing the environment will help minimize that fear. Consistent phone calls can help reduce the anxiety as well. Make a phone date with your child. For example call on Monday, Wednesday and Friday at 7:00 PM. (Of course, call at other times too—but make phone appointments to help generate consistency.)

THE EMOTION: ANGER

A child's anger may not be directed at any person in particular, but more at the situation as a whole. Displaced anger is common. Children may attempt to punish you, the other parent or a sibling as they try to deal with this strong emotion.

THE SIGNS

Common signs of an angry child include:
- A short temper
- A child who will get frustrated during a conversation and walk away
- A child who frequently raises his voice
- A child who quickly challenges his parents' advice or decisions
- A child who has problems in school fighting with peers or talking back to teachers

IDEAS TO WORK WITH

Try to find a way for your child to vent his anger such as a pillow fight, a punching bag, fast dance—anything that can use up his energy. It is important your child understands that feeling angry is okay. Help your child to find an acceptable means of expressing the anger.

Listen to your children. Many children will be too angry to talk to their parents. Be observant and take advantage of all opportunities to communicate.

Don't meet anger with anger. Showing your anger to a child will only increase the problem. Instead, let the child cool down, then go share rationally that you are upset with his behavior. Do not reward the angry child. Do not try to make up for the anger or "solve" it by giving in to his every desire. Do not buy things to compensate or give him more attention because of his actions. Doing these things will maintain his anger. He will learn that, by being angry, he will get his way.

Finally, if you feel that the anger is self-destructive, you will need to consult a professional.

THE EMOTION: JEALOUSY

When a parent moves into another relationship, a child may quickly become jealous. She may fear you are trying to replace the other parent. Many single parents are short on time. When that parent becomes involved with a new interest, her child may feel there will be little time left for her.

THE SIGNS

The signs of jealousy are usually quite apparent
•The child may become competitive
•The child may compare your new interest to her father or mother
•The child may become overbearing in seeking your attention
•The child may frequently interrupt any conversations that you have
  with a new interest
•The child may say outright that you love or care for your new
  interest more than her

IDEAS TO WORK WITH

Many parents simply avoid dating to avoid this problem. That is not the healthy answer. Your child can express her feelings about your dating life, but she should not control it.

Make sure that you're not spending too much time with your new interest. Don't have that person over on days you normally spend with your children. Instead choose one day that you will all spend together. The rest of the time, meet somewhere else. As your children grow used to another person in their lives, you can gradually increase the amount of time you all spend together.

THE EMOTION: FEAR

Children who live in a two-parent home expect to wake up every morning with two parents. Children become accustomed to this routine. When a routine is changed by the loss, divorce or separation of a parent, fear often arises. Children fear that since they have, in their mind, "lost" one parent they could easily lose the other as well.

THE SIGNS

Children who feel fear can display a wide variety of signs, some of the more common include:

- A child who constantly seeks reassurance that everything will be okay.
- A child who does not like to be separated from a parent, and becomes insecure when separated.
- A child who clams up and quits talking and does not want to discuss his fears.

> If your schedule allows, get involved WITH your child in activities (like coaching sports, for example.) This can actually expand your relationship with your child. The child sees you in a very different role.
>
> R.W.
> Los Gatos, California

IDEAS TO WORK WITH

Helping a child overcome his fears will greatly benefit the child. A child can overcome his fears by using one of two basic methods: expression or action.

Action involves trying to conquer the fear by confronting it. A child may feel fear when separated from a parent. To conquer the fear a child might begin by being away from the parent for thirty minutes, then increasing that time to an hour. The child would increase the time apart in small increments until he felt little fear in being separated.

Expression involves verbally working through the fear. A child would discuss with a parent, or other trusted adult, what he fears. The child would search for the source of that fear. The parent then uses questions to help the child put the fear into perspective.

Which method you use depends on your child. A verbal child will benefit most from the expression method whereas a child who is hands-on will benefit most from the action method.

Some fears may be too deep-rooted for the parent to offer the help that is needed. If you cannot reach your child's fear, seek help with a trained professional.

THE EMOTION: WITHDRAWAL

Children who withdraw may do so for a variety of reasons. Some children fear further pain and think that, if they do not show emotion, or attempt not to feel, they cannot be hurt. Other children withdraw out of anger in an attempt to shut out parents. Other children, who have witnessed fighting or abuse, withdraw in order to make themselves "disappear" from the hurt.

THE SIGNS

- A child talks less than usual and does not share her daily events
- The child may answer questions with short responses
- The child may spend as much time out of the house as possible or spend more time alone in his room
- The child may find new reasons to be away from the house, such as studying at the library or enrolling in new extracurricular interests

IDEAS TO WORK WITH

After any big change in a person's life, a certain amount of space is needed to sort through one's thoughts. Parents should be able to tell the difference between a healthy distance and withdrawal.

It is important that parents encourage and support a child who is withdrawn. Do not nag, yell or ridicule a withdrawn child—this may cause an adverse effect and the child may withdraw more.

Spending time together on a regular basis along with encouragement and support will help your child to open up.

If your child seems severely withdrawn he could be suffering from depression, alcohol abuse or drug abuse. In these instances, seek professional help.

EMOTION: REJECTION

Children cannot always understand that a divorce or separation is between the parents, not the child and the parent. Children may feel that they have been rejected or divorced by a parent. Hectic visitation schedules and short abrupt calls from the non-custodial parent can also leave the child feeling rejected. A parent spending time that used to be spent with a child, with a new interest can cause feelings of rejection as well.

> Listen, really listen, and show interest when with your child. You'd be surprised how much your kids will talk.
> *Julie McKay*
> *Glover, Vermont*

THE SIGNS

- A child compares his parents to one another and says things like "he or she likes me more"

- A child complains that "nobody likes me," or "no one ever has time for me"

- A child gets very upset when visitation plans are broken

- A child seems to suffer from low self-esteem

IDEAS TO WORK WITH

Reassure the child that you and your former partner have separated and this was not caused by the child. Keep affirming that, while your relationship has changed with the child's other parent, both parents' relationships and feelings toward the child remain unchanged.

Attempt to keep visitation times and phone calls frequent and on schedule. Make sure to take the time to hear out your child and truly listen to her concerns and fears.

There is a fine line between these emotions and their signs. Many of these signs and emotions will overlap. These signs should serve only as guidelines, and as always, if you have any serious worries or questions, consult a professional.

THE ART OF COMMUNICATION

Communication is the maker or breaker of all relationships. When adults have problems in personal or work-related areas, lack of communication is the cause nine times out of ten.

The same can be said for the parent and child relationship. "You just don't understand!" is a comment many parents hear. When I talk to children they often mention lack of communication with parents as a main problem.

Do not underestimate the importance of communication. Most problems and conflicts can be avoided or solved when two people take the time to share thoughts and feelings.

It is never too late to re-open the doors. It is never too early to begin forming good communication habits. If you are trying to rebuild rapport with a child, be prepared to give it a lot of time. When stronger ties are established, the effort will be worth every hour.

How do you establish positive communication? You learn new ways to listen and talk with your child.

SECRET SIGNS

Unfortunately, your child may not jump up and say "talk to me!" each time he seeks conversation. You will need to learn to recognize the secret signs that show your child is seeking conversation.

There are two common secret signs. The first is more often seen in younger children. A child will come up and tug on a parent's sleeve. This is often a sign that a child has something to say or is seeking attention. Many parents will turn to their child and say, "Quit pulling on my sleeve!" They are unaware that this reaction may hurt later communication.

A young child does not have many ways to let you know he needs your time. The times your child yearns for attention won't always be convenient. If a child seeks attention that you can't offer right away, respond with an alternative. For example, if you are on the phone or in conversation and a child pulls your sleeve, take a moment to pause and let the child know you will be available in two minutes.

The other secret sign is seen more in older children. They often enter a room and just sit down. They may not talk, but just seem to linger. Often, this can signal to a parent that there is something the child would like to talk about.

> Think before you speak or act, you can't take anything back.
> *Charlotte Smith*
> *Enfield, Connecticut*

Perhaps the child does not know how to lead into the conversation. An easy way to start conversation is to ask a specific question. For older children, try asking something specific about a television show or hobby. For example, "What did you think of last week's *Third Rock* episode?" For younger children, ask a specific question like, "How did the teacher like your science project at school?" or "What game did you play today in gym class? Who was on which team?" If you ask something like, "How was your day?" you will most likely be answered with, "fine." If you ask, "Is there anything you would like to talk about?" you will probably hear, "not really." Start with some specific, non-threatening questions and watch for your child's lead as he works his way towards the specific topic he wants to address.

THE FIVE RULES OF LISTENING

RULE #1 - Listen with your whole body.

When listening to your child remember the cliché, *action speaks louder than words.* Turn off the television, keep good eye contact, put down the paper and give your child your undivided attention.

RULE #2 - Ask questions.

Asking questions will show your child you're interested in what she has to say. It will also extend a conversation and open up more areas to talk about.

RULE #3 - Do not interrupt.

Plain and simple, do not interrupt. Let your child speak his mind.

RULE #4 - Don't have all the answers.

While children may come to you for answers, it is better to ask questions and encourage the child to find their own answers.

RULE #5 - Repeat, repeat, repeat.

Repeat what your child says. This will assure your child that you are listening and you will know you're understanding your child's message.

These five basic rules of listening will help you to get your communication lines open. Keep in mind, it will take time. If you have not had positive communication with your child, and your child suddenly finds you are all ears, your child may wonder what's up. Implement the five rules over time. Start with one and then add the others.

COMMUNICATION GAMES

You can open up communication doors by playing communication games. One favorite is a form of "20 questions."

You will need 20 index cards or pieces of paper, a couple of pens, a paper bag and two dice. To begin, each person writes down a set number of questions so that you have a total of 20. If there are two players, each player writes down ten, if there are 4 players, each player writes down five, etc.

The questions can be about anything the person would like to know. For example, "Is there anyone you would want to trade places with for a day? If so, who?" or "If you were at the family Christmas at Grandma's and you found a dead bug in your milk, would you say something?"

Next, mix all the questions together in a bag. Keep in mind, you may be answering your own questions—so be careful what you ask!

Roll the dice. Whoever rolls the lowest number picks a question and answers it. Continue rolling until all 20 questions have been answered.

TEN WAYS TO ENHANCE COMMUNICATION

1. Spend quality time together on a regular basis.
2. Relax around your children and talk truthfully.
3. Take the time to pick up secret signs.
4. Ask questions!
5. Show your child the same respect you show other people who you value.
6. Don't nag, interfere or command!
7. Observe your current habits and make sure you don't engage in habits that block communication.
8. Encourage and praise children.
9. Let children tell you their side of the story.
10. Express your love.

FIVE WAYS WE BLOCK COMMUNICATION

Being aware of ways to improve communication is a big step in opening communication lines. Yet parents also need to look at their current communication habits and make sure they are not *blocking* communication.

The following list shows five ways parents commonly cause rifts in communication. Check to see if any of these apply to your situation.

Waiting for the time to be right. Many times parents will wait for the perfect atmosphere to begin conversation. They tell their child, "We will talk after dinner," or "Let me just have a few minutes." By the time parents are ready, even if it is only a few minutes, a child may re-think what they were going to say. A parent will not hear the same story. There isn't always a right time. Take advantage of any time your child chooses to open up.

Not giving the child the benefit of the doubt. Parents will sometimes assume a scenario. If you assume something, you're denying the child an opportunity to tell her side of the story. This closes the door on communication. For, example, if your child comes home and says, "I was sent to the office today," and you reply, "You have to quit getting in trouble!" You are assuming the ending. Maybe your child got the most A's in class and got sent to the office to accept a new reward created in her honor! Okay, not likely. But, you won't know unless you ask. The key is to ask! Instead of the above, try something like, "Why did you get sent to the office?" or "Was it fair that you were sent to the office?" This shows the child that you feel they are responsible enough to tell you the true story and you value what they say.

Ordering Or Commanding A Child Children do need to be advised and guided in their actions. There are effective and non-effective ways of getting this guidance across. Let's take an example of a child who is supposed to take out the garbage. You have asked him twice and the garbage is still in the kitchen. Try an approach like, "John, I have asked you twice to take out the garbage. Is there any reason you haven't done it yet?" This question also needs to be stated in an even tone for it to be effective. By asking this question, you are offering your child a chance to explain his actions. Follow-up with the statement, "Could you please take it out now?" In many instances this will be enough to get the garbage taken out.

What many parents do is enter the room and see the garbage still sitting there and say something like, "John, take that garbage out right now!" or "I've asked you twice to take out the garbage—why haven't you done it yet?" By ordering your child, you're not offering communication like we did in the previous example.

The Nag. There is nothing that annoys children more than being nagged. The nagging parent will continually remind the child to get a desired result. Nagging undermines a child's self-esteem. Think about how we communicate as adults: we don't nag one another to get things done. Instead we ask each other. Ask your child, don't nag.

Interfering. If a child does not ask your opinion, they most likely don't want to know it. If a parent jumps in offering all their worldly advice, they are interfering in their child's own thought process. Instead of helping the child, this usually causes the child to think "Well, if I don't do it the way Mom or Dad would have done it, they might be mad." Instead of making decisions based on her own resources, a child is influenced by her parents.

Let your child make discoveries on her own. Don't jump in to solve every problem. Of course, there are some problems of a high magnitude where a parent should step in. Use your judgment.

SURVEY FINDINGS

We asked our survey participants to rank how they felt about the following statement, "I feel my child has dealt well with upsetting emotions about living in a single-parent family." Here is what they said:

Five (strongly disagree)	7%
Four	15%
Three	26%
Two	23%
One (strongly agree)	24%
No opinion	5%

SINGLE PARENTS WORDS OF WISDOM
ON COMMUNICATION WITH CHILDREN

"Be careful not to spoil your children every time you feel they get over-emotional or frustrated about living in a single-parent home.

Yes, your children are living in a different home environment, but this alone does not make them different from other children. They need to know they do not need "special" gifts or extra "attention" in order to compensate for their unique family situation."

C.L.P.

San Jose, California

"Keep a short list of close friends that are nearby, who are willing to relieve you in an escalating stressful time—like baby crying forever. Just ten minutes of quiet can help you calm down enough to regain control of your own emotions and better deal with the situation."

Judith Ashbaugh

Murphysboro, Illinois

"Take time to giggle with your children."

Lisa Jenkins

Montgomery, Alabama

"Involve your children in your relationships with other single-parent families so they can also know that they are not alone in their life situation, and in their feelings and concerns."

J. Mower

Salt Lake City, Utah

"Be sure to admit to your children when you make mistakes. If they think you are perfect then they will think that they have to be perfect too."

Single Mother

Columbus, Ohio

"Hug your child often; (s)he needs it...and so do you!"

Karen E. Clark
Morgantown, West Virginia

"Love your child unconditionally, but don't let your child control your life."

Single Mother
Tacoma, Washington

"Teach your child the art of conversation. Even the very young benefit from learning prompted exchange."

Single Mother of Internationally adopted daughter
Rochester Hills, Michigan

"Don't push your child away or tell them 'later' because there is something else that needs to be done."

Michelle Harmon
Gresham, Oregon

"Enjoy your child (even a colicky baby looks and smells like an angel when they are asleep!)"

M.B.
Dallas, Texas

"Put yourself in your child's shoes and ask how you might deal with these issues at their age."

Shelley Brockelbank
Gloucester, Ontario

"Enjoy each moment with your child. Don't keep waiting for the future, live now. Laugh with your child and play with your child. The chores will always be there."

Maria Kleinbub
Maspeth, New York

"Be consistent… in everything! Routines, not giving in to tantrums, family traditions (old and new), explanations, etc."

Single Mother of Internationally adopted daughter
Rochester Hills, Michigan

"Listen to yourself and trust yourself. You know your child best."

Patricia Flint, single mother of twins
Glastonbury, Connecticut

"Keep an open line of communication with your children. Be their parent first and then their best friend."

Sophia A. Evans
Bryans Road, Maryland

"Let your children know that if you all work together, you will all "make it." Don't let them use the divorce as an excuse for behaving badly. Don't you use it as an excuse for letting children "get by" with inappropriate behavior, either."

N.F.
Hunstville, Alabama

"Set up an opportunity for your child to have a "significant adult other" in his or her life who will always be there (in other words—not someone you are dating, but a friend.) I asked two male friends to take over as "godparents" when my ex-husband moved across country. I do not date either of these men and they have been with us through many good times and bad. They will often attend events that my daughter participates in or even show up for "Father's Day" celebrations at school. She knows they will always be there."

S.S.

Huntsville, Alabama

"As soon as you get home spend 15-20 minutes of focused, attentive time with your children before beginning dinner, chores, etc."

Single Mother of Internationally adopted daughter

Rochester Hills, Michigan

"Be active in providing your children examples or role models for knowledge, spirituality, morality and civility."

Keevin Allen

Oconomowoc, Wisconsin

"Find ways to make time productive for both you and your child. For example, while I study, my son colors at the same table (very quietly of course)."

Joshua K. Blair

State College, Pennsylvania

"You don't have to do everything it says in those advice books on raising children to have a healthy family. Just let your children know you love them."

Judy Barker

Chandler, Arizona

"Children are children for a limited time and they learn from us how to be adults. Be a good role model."

Single Mom

Boise, Idaho

"Although my daughter gets special attention, she knows there are limits to what she can get away with. Parents need to set those boundaries. As a single parent, it is sometimes hard to do that."

Christine Kuriger

Norman, Oklahoma

"Be cautious not to do or say anything that pulls the child into conflicts with a former partner."

Eileen Argentina

Eugene, Oregon

"Don't hide things from your children. They understand a lot more than you might think. Don't use them as "listening boards," but DO explain to them what is going on."

M.R.

Margate, Florida

"Children are our most precious gift and have the ability to do great things. Let your children feel loved and cared for—in turn you are giving them the confidence to accomplish anything!"

Single Mother

Canada

RESOURCES FOR CHILDREN'S EMOTIONAL HEALTH

ALCOHOL

Alateen is part of the Al-Anon Family Groups, "the fellowship of people whose lives are being, or have been affected, by close contact with a problem drinker. Alateens get together at meetings to help each other with the problems they have in common. They share their experiences, learn about alcoholism, the family disease, and concentrate on their personal growth in order to lessen the harmful effects of alcoholism on their lives. They do this by studying and applying to themselves the Twelve Steps adopted from Alcoholics Anonymous. As the name implies, Alateen is designed for members in their teens. Family members below teen years may not be ready for the Alateen program. There are, however, younger children who can benefit from the Alateen program which requires the ability to participate in a shared learning experience." Alateen offers a free introductory packet of literature. Call (800) 356-9996 in the United States or (800) 714-7498 in Canada. For meeting information call (800) 344-2666 in the United States and (800) 443-4525 in Canada. You can also visit their web sites at:

http://www.alateen.org,

http://www.al-anon.alateen.org

http://www.al-anon.org

ANGER

Dealing with the Angry Child. This 2 page brochure offers practical advice to help parents reinforce positive behavior and help children express anger appropriately. This free brochure is item 630D—send your request to Consumer Information Center, Pueblo, CO 81009.

DEPRESSION

please see resources listed in Chapter Six

DRUG INFORMATION AND HELP

Growing Up Drug Free shows parents what children should know about drugs, including alcohol and tobacco, at each age level. This 33 page brochure is free. Request item 505D from the Consumer Information Center, Pueblo, CO 81009.

Schools Without Drugs is a free, 91 page brochure that provides an action plan for parents, teachers, school administrators and students to help fight drug use. Request brochure 510D from the Consumer Information Center, Pueblo, CO 81009.

For information on treatment and recovery see SUBSTANCE ABUSE AND RECOVERY in the Additional Resource section at the close of this book.

EATING DISORDERS

Eating Disorders. Learn symptoms, possible medical complications, treatments, how to help and resources for more information. This 17 page brochure is available for .50 cents. from the Consumer Information Center, Pueblo, CO 81009.

Grace Square Hospital Eating Disorder Hotline (800) 382-2832

Bulimia, Anorexia Self Help, Behavior Adaption Support and Healing
(800) 762-3334
(800) 227-4785

HELP LINES

Youth Crisis Hotline (800) HIT-HOME

Christian counselors can offer counseling for any problems you are facing.

Children's Rights of America   (800) 422-HOPE

"Need help? There's hope." Call this hotline for questions about abuse, suicide, self-esteem, gangs and any other problem.

RUNAWAYS

The National Runaway Switchboard   (800)-621-4000

This 24 hour hotline can offer help to those who are (or know someone) who is on the run or thinking about running away from home. Parents can also receive counseling at this number.

Children of the Night   (800) 551-1300

Runaways can call the counselors at this 24 hour help line for counseling or referrals to shelters and health care services.

SUICIDE

National Adolescent Suicide Hotline   (800) 621-4000

American Association of Suicidology (AAS)

The goal of this organization is to understand and prevent suicide. They serve as a national clearinghouse on information about suicide. Contact them at 4201 Connecticut Ave., NW, Suite 310, Washington, DC 20008. Or call (202) 237-2280

SUCCESS IN SCHOOL

Helping Your Child Succeed in School. This 52 page brochure offers 15 fun activities to do with children ages 5-11. These activities will help expand their imagination, obey, organize, help others and much more. Request the brochure from the Consumer Information Center, Pueblo, CO 81009. Request item 311D and include a check for .50 cents.

YOUTH LAW

The National Center for Youth Law "is a nonprofit national support center for legal services, lawyers and other advocates working on behalf of low-income children and adolescents nationwide. NCYL provides technical assistance, specialized legal expertise and publications, training and serves as a co-counsel on cases of broad impact." The following information is available: general organizational brochure; *Fair Housing For Families Project*; *The Basics of California's Child Support System*; fact sheets on *Children's Suplemental Security Income (SSI) program*; *California Children's SSI Resource Guide*. For information write to: National Center for Youth Law, 114 Sansome Street, Suite 900, San Francisco, CA 94104-3820. You can visit their web site at *http://www.youthlaw.org* or e-mail them at *info@youthlaw.org*

CHAPTER TWELVE
MYTHS AND MUDSLINGING
SLAMMING THE DOOR
ON THE NEGATIVES AND
OPENING THE DOOR TO A
MORE POSITIVE LIFE

Before we jump into the material in this chapter, I want to share my own feelings about the data and how I chose what to include. Basically, I found single parents in the survey were often haunted by stereotypes—many of which could not be documented. I wanted to relay data that I felt came from reliable and objective sources. And I wanted you to be able to interpret that data for yourself—therefore, I have offered little interpretation.

Another area of single-parenting that I find troublesome is the need to condemn one group or another for the issues and problems of society. Throughout my research for this book, I found many groups condemning single mothers for the state of the nation and equal numbers of groups condemning single fathers. The numbers used to back these claims were interpreted in such a way that the factual element was often skewed.

We must identify issues and concerns in order to help and improve the nation's single-parent families. We don't need to argue about who is best at this or that, or who is wrong or right—we need to be vehicles for change, not vehicles for confrontation.

As I read about single mothers blaming single fathers, single fathers blaming single mothers and society blaming anyone single—I was left with some questions. What if single parents quit blaming and worked together to inform and change society's perception of the single-parent family? How would that benefit our kids? And isn't that more important than being right or wrong? As for disagreements on who is better suited to raise a child— the mom or dad—who is the deadbeat—I listed only the facts. You can interpret the data from there and make your own judgments.

Because much of the information I attempted to verify from groups and other sources was inaccurate or taken out of context, I have supplied only statistics gathered from the Census Bureau or the National Center of Health Statistics.

My overview is this—children deserve relationships with both their mother and father when healthy and possible. Children deserve parents who can put aside their own anger and work toward this goal.

STATISTICS ABOUT THE SINGLE-PARENT FAMILY

- Most single parents have either never been married or are currently divorced. In 1994 about 38% of single parents were never married, and about an equal share were divorced. These two categories combined accounted for three of every four single parents. The remainder were either married but not living with their spouse (20%) or widowed (5%). - Steve W. Rawlings, Households and Families report of the U.S. Census Bureau.

- One out of two or 32.3 million American children lived in a situation other than the "traditional nuclear family" in 1991. - Bureau of the Census, 1994

- The U.S. divorce rate is nearly twice as high as those in other industrialized countries. - Population Reference Bureau, Inc., March 1996

- The largest proportional increase of any marital status category occurred among divorced persons. The number of currently divorced persons more than tripled from 4.3 million in 1970 to 15.8 million in 1991, representing nine percent of all adults age 18 and over in 1991. - Bureau of the Census

- Between 1970 and 1991, the proportion of children in two-parent living arrangements declined from 85 percent to 72 percent while the proportion of children living with one parent more than doubled from 12 percent to 26 percent. - Bureau of the Census

- Sixty-one percent of all children will spend all or part of their formative years in a single parent household. - Bureau of the Census

- Married couples' weekly earnings ($783) continued to be about 25 percent higher than those of families maintained by men ($520) and twice as much as the earnings of single-parent families headed by women ($385). - Bureau of the Census

- The proportion of single-parent families has increased. The percent of all parent-child family groups maintained by single parents rose from 13 percent in 1970 to 30 percent in 1993. Nearly three-fourths of these "single" parents either had never married or were divorced. - Bureau of the Census, 1995.

- A child in a one-parent situation was just slightly more likely to be living with a divorced parent (37 percent) in 1993 than with a never-married parent (35 percent). A decade ago, a child living with one parent was almost twice as likely to be living with a divorced parent than with a never-married parent. - 1994 Report from the Commerce Department's Census Bureau

- Although two-thirds of all single parents are White, one-parent situations are much more common among African Americans. About 63 percent of all African American family groups with children were maintained by single parents, versus 25 percent of comparable White family groups. Among Hispanics, single parents represented 35 percent of family groups with children. - March Annual Demographic Supplement to the Current Population Survey, Bureau of the Census, 1994

- The average number of persons in a household was 2.63 in 1993. - Bureau of the Census 1994

- Two-parent families accounted for 36 percent of family households in 1993, down from 50 percent in 1970. - March Annual Demographic Supplement to the Current Population Survey, Bureau of the Census, 1994

- First marriages ending in divorce lasted an average of 11 years for both men and women, while remarriages ending in divorce last an average of 7.4 years for men and 7.1 years for women. Nationally, all marriages ending in divorce lasted an average of 9.8 years. - National Center for Health Statistics, Advance Report of Final Divorce Statistics 1980 and 1990.

- The number of married persons has increased from 95 million to 114.5 million between 1970 and 1993, although the increase in unmarried adults was greater (from 37.5 million to 72.6 million). The number of never-married persons doubled from 21.4 million to 42.3 million during the same time period, and account for the largest share of unmarried adults. - Bureau of the Census, 1994

- Over the last two decades, the number of women living alone rose 94 percent (from 7.3 to 14.2 million), while the number of men living alone rose 167 percent (from 3.5 million to 9.4 million). - Bureau of the Census, 1994.

- Approximately 4.7 million children live with a grandparent. Most children (81 percent) who lived with a single parent and grandparent lived in the grandparent's home, but most children (62 percent) living with two parents and a grandparent lived in the parents' home. - The Census Bureau's Survey of Income and Program Participation, 1994

- Among children in single-mother families, one-fifth also had an adult male (related or unrelated) present in the household; about two-fifths of children living with a single father also had an adult female (related or unrelated) living with them. The other adult may be, for example, the child's grandparent, aunt, uncle, or cousin. - The Census Bureau's Survey of Income and Program Participation, 1994

FACTS ABOUT SINGLE MOTHERS
Highlights from The National Center for Health Statistics report Births to Unmarried Mothers: United States, 1980-92.

- One of every three births in America is to an unmarried mother.
- In 1992 there were 1.2 million births to unmarried women, almost double the number in 1980. The most pronounced increase was for white women aged 20 and over.
- The rate of non-marital childbearing rose 54 percent among women ages 15-44 between 1980 and 1992.
- The largest increase among birth rates to unmarried women is among women over 20. Consequently, only 30 percent of unmarried women giving birth in 1992 were teenagers.
- Since 1980, the non-marital birth rate for white women rose 94 percent and the rate for black women increased only 7 percent, causing a dramatic decline in the disparity of unmarried parents by race.
- The number of children living only with their mother grew from 5.1 million in 1960 to 16.3 million in 1994. Marital Status and Living Arrangements, 1994. U.S. Bureau of the Census, Current Population Reports.

From the U.S. Census Bureau's Facts for Mother's Day, 1997
- In 1993, 73.9 of the Nation's 103.4 million women 15 years old and over were mothers.

- Of the 73.9 million mothers, 23 percent have given birth to one child during their lifetimes, 35 percent to two children, 21 percent to three, 11 percent to four and 10 percent to five or more.

- The median age of women who gave birth in 1993 was 26.4 years; those giving birth for the first time were 23.8 years. These median ages were 1.0 and 1.7 years older respectively than they were 20 years earlier.

- In 1995, there were nearly 10 million single mothers with children under 18.

- Of the 22.8 million never-married women 15 to 44 years old in 1995, 21 percent were mothers.

FACTS ABOUT SINGLE FATHERS

SURVEY FINDINGS
We asked our survey participants to rate how they felt about the following statement on a scale of one to five. "I feel my child is doing better in a single-parent family than he/she would have in our prior family arrangement." Here is what they said:
Five (strongly disagree) 11%
Four 11%
Three 14%
Two 11%
One (strongly agree) 50%
No opinion 3%

- Between 1970 and 1980 there was little or no change in the proportion of single parent children living with their father (from 9.1 percent to 8.5 percent). Between 1980 and 1991 the rate rose to 12.1 percent. - Bureau of the Census

- Some 40% of America's children do not live with their biological fathers.

From the U.S. Census Bureau's Facts for Father's Day, 1997.

- In 1995, 2.5 million children (4 percent) lived with their father, but not their mother. Among these children's fathers, 48 percent were divorced, 28 percent had never been married, 18 percent were married but not living with their wife and five percent were widowed.

FACTS ABOUT CHILD SUPPORT

- 5.5 million women and 648,000 men were awarded child support in 1991. 76% of these women got some or all payments due. 63% of these men got some or all due. The women got an average of $3000 from non-custodial fathers. The men got an average of $2300 from non-custodial mothers. - Bureau of the Census

- Out of 5.7 million women who were due child support in 1989, only 50 percent of the women received full payment while 25 percent received no payments. Bureau of the Census.

- 91% of fathers who got joint custody in 1994 paid full child support. - Bureau of the Census

- Parents due child support in 1991 received only 67 percent or $11.9 billion of the $17.7 billion due them. -Commerce Department's Census Bureau and the Department of Health and Human Services, 1995.

Other statistics from the Bureau of the Census:

- Of 11.5 million custodial parents in the United States in the spring 1992, 6.2 million had been awarded child support with 5.3 million parents due to receive payments in 1991. 1.6 million of these were custodial fathers, 400,000 of whom were due payments in 1991. Nearly five million custodial mothers expected child support.

- Custodial mothers were awarded child support at a higher rate than fathers— 56 percent as compared to 41 percent.

- According to a 1989 Census Bureau study, 90 percent of fathers with joint custody pay child support on time and in full. Almost 80 percent of fathers with visitation arrangements do as well.

- Reasons given by custodial mothers for not receiving child support were:

   Did not pursue the award 35%

   Unable to locate father 21%

Father financially unable to pay 16%

One third of custodial fathers who did not receive child support in 1991 stated they did not want an award; one-third said they did not pursue it and about one-fifth said the mother was unable to pay.

- Approximately 38 percent of custodial mothers and 15 percent of custodial fathers contacted a government agency for assistance in obtaining child support.

FACTS ABOUT CHILD CUSTODY

- In 19 reporting States, 72 percent of custody cases were awarded to the wife, and 9 percent of custody cases were awarded to the husband. Joint custody was awarded in 16 percent of the cases. - National Center for Health Statistics, Advance Report of Final Divorce Statistics 1980 and 1990.

THOUGHTS FROM SINGLE PARENTS

"Never feel guilty about the fact that you are a single parent. A healthy one parent relationship is better than a dysfunctional two parent relationship."

Stacy De Carlo
San Jose, California

"Be confident in yourself and your family. You are not inferior. No one has the right to judge you."

Single Mother
Baltimore, Maryland

"Hold your head up and keep going."

Amanda Cook
Germantown, Tennessee

"If you are comfortable with your situation, your child will be also."

K.R.

Brookline, Massachusetts

"Develop confidence in your parenting skills, take courses, attend classes, etc. When there is no positive support around, this will be essential to your self-esteem. When all the stress of a single parent's life get you down, at least you will be able to look yourself in the mirror and tell yourself you are doing a great job parenting. I have found this to be my greatest source of self-nourishment."

Single Mother

Toronto, Canada

"Don't accept that children in single-parent families have more problems than other kids. Be a good role model and expect your child to do well socially and academically and they have the same chance as children from two-parent families."

Mary J. Waddell

"Don't let other people's opinions haunt you."

Jen Larsoin

Newark, Deleware

SURVEY FINDINGS

We asked our survey participants if they felt children in single-parent homes could grow up to be at least as well adjusted as children raised in a traditional two-parent home.

Using five to strongly disagree and one to strongly agree, here is what they said:

Five (strongly disagree)	6%
Four	14%
Three	22%
Two	24%
One (strongly agree)	30%
No opinion	4%

"Don't buy into the myth that single parents "can't" [cope, raise decent children, have dignity, etc.] We can. And we do."

Sheridan Massey

Australia

THE SINGLE PARENT FAMILY
HOW WE HINDER
HOW WE HELP

If the statistics above tell us anything, it's that the single-parent family form is here to stay and the number of single-parent families is growing at a rapid rate. While the arguments of whether children are better off in a one-parent or two-parent family will probably go on forever, it is not my focus to argue one case or the other. I believe that any family form can nurture and raise happy and healthy children as long as love and respect are present. Likewise, I believe any family form can be detrimental to a child's upbringing when there is an absence of love or respect.

There are ways that we as a society currently hinder the growth of the single-parent family as it makes its journey to a recognized and accepted family form.

SURVEY FINDINGS

When asked how our single parent survey respondents thought society perceived the single parent family, they reported the following:

The same as the two-parent traditional family.   1%

A new kind of family that is opening people's eyes to different kinds of successful family arrangements.
                                                            14%

A family with more problems than most.
                                                            40%

A family inferior to the traditional nuclear family.
                                                            43%

No opinion   2%

To educate and understand is the key to changing the outdated view much of society holds. To successfully accomplish this, I believe it is vital that single parents—both men and women—begin working together in raising and educating their children and their peers.

Many of the single parents surveyed felt that the media portrayed them in a dim light. They reported feeling inferior and that their children were often pre-sentenced by the media to less than desirable outcomes. One step we can take together is to share stories of success as single parents and band together to ensure these stories get equal coverage in the media.

We also need to be advocates for acceptance in our schools. So much of what our children learn, feel and interpret comes from peers. Making the time to become involved in our school systems is vital to changing the face of the American family. Begin support groups. Talk to teachers and make sure they aren't using lingo like "broken homes." As children learn more and more about sex and the danger in our school systems, become an advocate of starting a short-term evening class that teaches about love, parenting and different family forms. Ask that "mother & daughter" outings or "father & son" outings be changed to "parent & child" outings. Make sure that our children are not isolated within an environment where they should feel confident, welcome and safe.

SURVEY FINDINGS

We asked our survey participants to rate on a scale of one to five, (one being strongly agree, five being strongly disagree), how they felt about the following statement. "I feel my community accepts single-parent families."
Here is what they said:

Five (strongly disagree)	10%
Four	18%
Three	32%
Two	23%
One (strongly agree)	14%
No opinion	3%

In the same way, we need to educate ourselves and create support networks in our communities and our workplaces. While peers or the media may have pre-written the outcome of the single-parent home, it is up to us to dispel these negatives by maintaining a positive focus and not accepting society's wrongly-laid script. Encourage change in your workplace if it does not acknowledge or embrace families or the single-parent family. Pass around a flyer for a parents group to meet one lunch hour each week. Work together to share resources, car pooling, stories and triumphs. Make a voice for your family form.

Standing up proudly is another way to help disarm the grip of stereotypes on the single-parent family. There is no shame in being a single parent—no matter how you came to be one. You are a parent, a loving parent, that is what matters. Be open to questions about your family form and correct people around you when they interpret or misconstrue information.

We must also learn to quit using blame as a cop-out for avoiding change. As single parents, we can blame the fathers or the mothers, the media or the government, the traditional family, or the educational institution at large. Yet, every ounce of energy we give to blame is an ounce less that we have to devote to change. No one moves forward through blame—we only stall ourselves. While statistics can sway one group as the antagonists of a problem, pointing our fingers accomplishes nothing, instead, we need to offer our hand.

Likewise, the victim mentality must be dispelled so that we have the energy to make the advancements that are necessary. Holding ourselves as the victims of our situation will not change our situation, nor will it change the views of society. At some level, we are all responsible for our situation. When we let go of the victim mentality, we can empower ourselves to make the changes this society so desperately needs.

Only through our hard work at rewriting the endings of these scripts, can we create a track record that will allow the media to portray us in a positive light. We can change the statistics of single-parent homes at large. Through these changes, single-parent families will gain confidence in their ability to raise healthy, productive, well-adjusted children.

It is my sincere hope that through this book, and through touring and workshops, I can encourage single parents and others to embrace this family form. I hope you will do the same. Then, hopefully, in a revision of this book down the road, the statistics reported in this chapter will be different. What a joy that would be to read—for you, me, society—and most of all, for our children.

A CLOSING NOTE

I want to share a rather obvious story, but a story that still humors me nonetheless. I suffer from an ailment called chrondomalasia which is basically a sports injury affecting knee cartilage. It causes extreme pain and swelling when certain activities are performed or if I sit too long. Well, I had suffered from this for years and complained about it often. Finally, a friend asked if I had ever been treated, to which I replied that I hadn't.

The obvious suggestion was made to see a doctor. So I made my appointment, was told about chrondomalasia, given an exercise regimen to build up the muscles around my knees, and prescribed high doses of ibuprofen which I was to take daily for three weeks.

Three months passed and I was speaking to this same friend. Once again I was experiencing immense pain in my knees and began to utter complaints. He looked at me a bit dumbfounded. "The medication didn't work?"

"Well," I replied somewhat meekly, "I didn't take it all. "

"How much did you take?"

I could already feel myself blushing. I was supposed to take three caplets a day—instead I had taken three total. "Three. "

"Oh," he said with a knowing smirk. "And the exercises—how have you been doing with those?" He already knew the answer.

"Not so well," I confirmed. At this point we had no choice but to break into mutual laughter.

The point is that I went through the motions to improve my health—but I didn't follow through. I learned what I needed to do to improve my life, but I never put the ideas into action. Imagine how much better I felt when I completed the prescription and incorporated the exercises into my life. It demanded I create time that I didn't want to spare, but it was time well spent.

Can you make that same commitment with the ideas in this book? We have come as far as we can in sharing the knowledge gathered from single parents and experts. You have come as far as you can in reading the knowledge we have to share. You have had the commitment and willpower to learn practical strategies for improving your day-to-day life. Now it's up to you to implement them. Take a moment now to thumb through this book—go back to chapter one and see what you identified as your prime concerns and challenges. Find the chapters that offer advice. Contact the appropriate resources. Make a plan and follow through.

I hope you will. You're worth it.

ADDITIONAL RESOURCES

ADOPTION

The National Council for Single Adoptive Parents is an information service for single people interested in adoption in the US. They publish *The Handbook for Single Adoptive Parents*, describing how to go about adopting and how to manage as a single parent. The book is $20 including postage and handling. To order the book or request a brochure about the council and/or information on the handbook, write to: National Council for Single Adoptive Parents, PO Box 15084, Chevy Chase, MD 20825.

North American Council on Adoptable Children (NACAC) "believes every child has the right to a permanent family. The Council advocates the right of every child to a permanent, continuous, nurturing and culturally sensitive family, and presses for the legal adoptive placement of any child denied that right." Individual, family and parent memberships are $40 per year. They offer many informational sheets upon request. These include a general informational brochure, *How to Adopt: The Basics, Special Need Adoption Contacts, NACAC State and Provincial Representatives*, publication lists, membership benefits and more. For more information write to: NACAC, 970 Raymond Avenue, Suite 106, St. Paul, MN 55114-1149. Or visit their web site at *http://www.cyfc.mn.edu/Adoptinfo/nacac.html*

International Concerns for Children "is an organization that works to acquaint the concerned public with various ways to provide assistance to homeless children, education for those interested personally and professionally about procedures, inform prospective parents of the availability of "waiting children" in foreign countries and the United States. ICC publishes the annual *Report on Intercountry Adoption* with monthly updates. This book includes approximate costs, waiting periods, and types of children available from dozens of agencies and other organizations that ICC believes work in morally, ethically and legally correct ways for adoptive placement in North American Homes. It includes requirements for parents, single-parent information, I-600 orphan visa procedure, medical issues, coping with children's adjustment, a bibliography of useful books, etc. The ICC also maintains an *Adoption Photolisting* (12 month subscription with monthly updates) for children still in their birth countries for whom agencies are seeking adoptive homes." They also offer personal counseling, publish a quarterly newsletter and distribute several papers. The above mentioned services range from $2.50-$20.00. For information write to: International Concerns for Children, 911 Cypress, Boulder, CO 80303-2821. E-mail *ICC@boulder.net*

American Academy of Adoption Attorneys "is a national association of attorneys who practice, or have otherwise distinguished themselves, in the field of adoption law. The Academy's work includes promoting the reform of adoption lawyers and disseminating information on ethical adoption practices." A membership directory is available for $7. For more information or to obtain a directory, write to: American Academy of adoption Attorneys, PO Box 33053, Washington, DC 20033-0053. Or visit their web site at *http://www.adoptionattorneys.org*

National Adoption Information Clearinghouse compiles the most up-to-date adoption information available and disseminates it to adoption researchers, practitioners and the public. Call their toll free number for an introductory package (888) 251-0075.

AIDS AND SEXUALLY TRANSMITTED DISEASES (STD)

National AIDS Information Clearinghouse   (800) 874-5231

Center for Disease Control, National STD Hotline (800) 227-8922

National Aids Hotline   (800) 342-AIDS

The AIDS hotline offers information on the prevention, testing and treatment of HIV/AIDS.

CHILD ABUSE AND DOMESTIC VIOLENCE

National Child Abuse Hotline (800) 4-A-CHILD

National Council on Child Abuse and Family Violence

This helpline offers both assistance and counseling referrals regarding child, partner and elder abuse. (800) 222-2000

National Organization for Victim Assistance (800) TRY-NOVA

NOVA counselors can offer information and referrals as well as crisis counseling services for victims of abuse, family violence and sexual assault. This 24 hour national hotline offers information and referrals for women who are abused verbally, mentally or physically.

National Clearinghouse on Child Abuse & Neglect (800) FYI-3366

National Resource Center on Sexual Abuse (800) 543-7006

National Committee to Prevent Child Abuse (312) 663-3520

National Resource Center on Child Abuse & Neglect

(800) 227-5242

DISABILITIES

Blind Children's Center (800) 222-3566

IBM National Support Center for Persons with Disabilities

(800) 426-2133

National Alliance of Blind Students (800) 424-8666

National Information Center for Children and Youth with

Disabilities (800) 999-5599

National Alliance for Parents of the Visually Impaired

(800) 562-6265

National Center for Youth with Disability (800) 333-6293

National Center for Stuttering (800) 221-2483

National Information Clearinghouse for Infants with Disabilities

and Life-threatening Conditions (800) 922-1107

The Deafness Research Foundation (800) 535-3323

GRANDPARENTS

It is estimated that nearly four million children currently live in a household headed by a grandparent. For over one-third of these children no parent is present, and the grandparent assumes the role of primary caregiver to his or her grandchildren or great-grandchildren. The American Association of Retired Persons (AARP) established the Grandparent Information Center (GIC) to provide information and resource to help grandparents cope with their primary care giving roles. The Center is working with national and community-based agencies in the child care, aging, legal, and family services field to address this rapidly emerging phenomenon. For further information, contact AARP Grandparent Information Center, 601 E. NW, Washington, DC 20049. Phone: (202) 434-2296.

GRIEF

See resources in Chapter Six.

HEALTH

Civitex offers information on a broad range of problems from alcoholism to homelessness to family problems.   (800) 223-6004

Rural Information Center Heath Service offers referrals in rural areas.
(800) 633-7701

National Maternal and Child Health Clearinghouse
(703) 821-8955 ext. 254

National Center for Education in Maternal and Child Health
(703) 524-7802

The National Health Information Center (NHIC) is a health information referral service. NHIC links consumers and health professionals who have health questions to organizations best able to provide answers. NHIC was established in 1979 by the Office of Disease Prevention and Health Promotion (ODPHP) within the Public Health Service, US Department of Health and Human Services. The Center maintains an online directory of more than 1,100 health related organizations that can provide health information.

They include Federal and State agencies, voluntary associations, self-help and support groups, trade associations and professional societies. For service write to: The National Health Information Center, PO Box 1133, Washington, DC 20013-1133. Or call (800) 336-4797. Or e-mail *nhicinfo@health.org* Or visit their web site at *http://nhic-nt.health.org* or *http://nhic-net.health.org/nmp/conf.html* or *http://www.healthfinder.gov*

ILLNESS

American Diabetes Association, Inc.	(800) 342-2383
Juvenile Diabetes Foundation	(800) 223-1138
Candlelighters Childhood Cancer Foundation Center	(800) 366-2223
Cancer Information Service	(800) 422-6237
Epilepsy Foundation of America	(800) 332-1000

National Information Clearinghouse for Infants with Disabilities and Life-threatening Conditions (800) 922-1107

The National Organization for Rare Disorders, Inc. (NORD) "is a unique federation of voluntary health organizations dedicated to helping people with rare "orphan" diseases and assisting the organizations that serve them. NORD is committed to the identification, treatment, and cure of rare disorders through programs of education, advocacy, research and service." NORD provides information on over 5,000 rare diseases. NORD's newsletter, *Orphan Disease Update* is mailed three times a year. Dues are $30 annually and include a free report. For information call, write or fax: National Organization for Rare Disorders (NORD), PO Box 8923, New Fairfield, Connecticut, 06812. Phone (800) 999-6673. E-mail *orphan@nord-rdb.com* Or visit their web site at: *http://www.NORD-RDB.com/~orphan*

LEARNING DISABILITIES

Learning Disabilities Association of America (LDA) is a national nonprofit organization concerned with learning disabilities. They provide information through a free packet of material and offer referrals to one of their 500 local chapters. You can request an information packet by writing with the information you are seeking (i.e. ADD/ADHD, Dyslexia, the IEP, etc.) Send your request to: Learning Disabilities Association of America, 4156 Library Road, Pittsburgh, PA 15234-1349. Or visit their web site at *http://www.ldanatl.org*

MISSING CHILDREN

Family Protection Network, Inc. has a child registration and missing child search service called Child Team. Annual membership is $50 per child. For more information call   (800) 994-4199

Vanished Children's Alliance helps victims, conducts investigations, has counselors and more.   (800) VANISHED

Child Find helps locate children as well as helping lost children. Also has information for parents who have abducted their children in violation of a court order.   (800) A WAY OUT

National Center for Missing & Exploited Children helps locate missing children and offers information on missing and exploited youth.   (800) 843-5678

SAFETY

The National Crime Prevention Council offers assorted brochures to help keep kids safe. Some local police departments carry these brochures. Check with your local police department or write: The National Crime Prevention Council, 1700 K. Street, N.W., Second Floor, Washington, DC 20006.

SELF-HELP CLEARINGHOUSES

See resource section of Chapter Six.

SUBSTANCE ABUSE AND RECOVERY

Al-Anon Family Group Headquarters   (800) 356-9996
Alcoholism and Drug Treatment Addiction Center (800) 383-4357

American Council on Alcoholism   (800) 527-5344
800 Cocaine   (800) 262-2463
Just Say No, International   (800) 258-2766
National Clearinghouse for Alcohol and Drug Information
                                                  (800) 729-6686
National Drug and Alcohol Treatment Hotline   (800) 662-HELP

TRAVEL

Carousel Press is a publisher of travel books designed to assist parents
in planning their vacation. They publish a catalog *The Family Travel
Guide*, which is filled with helpful family-oriented travel guides and
children's travel activity books. You can receive a free copy of this
catalog by sending a self addressed stamped envelope to: Carousel
Press, PO Box 6038, Albany, CA 94706-0038.

VITAL RECORDS

Where to Write for Vital Records is a page at the MedAccess Internet
site. It lists different vital records and what is needed to obtain
them. *http://www.medaccess.com/address/vital_toc.htm*

WELFARE

"Welfare Warriors is a multiracial group of mothers in poverty who
have had to receive public child support (welfare). Their mission is
to create a voice for mothers in poverty—through media and grass
roots organizing—so that decisions affecting families will be made
by those with actual experience and knowledge of the problems." A
membership is $15 for an individual, $4 for victims of poverty.
Send a SASE for their publication list and information sheets on
poverty and welfare. Write to: Welfare Warriors, 2711 W. Michigan, Milwaukee, WI 53208.

WOMEN

Woman Magazine is a bimonthly collection of fiction, poetry and self-help columns of special interest to women. "Our goal is empowerment through education." A one year subscription is $16.95. Send subscription requests to: *Woman Magazine*, Post Office Box 438, Meadville, Pennsylvania, 16335.

APPENDIX
SURVEY METHODOLOGY AND FINDINGS

The contents of *The Single Parent Resource* are based in substantial part on a survey of 500 single parents.

This is a self-selected survey. The question that immediately comes to mind about this (or any other) genre of research is: How valid is it? Do the findings accurately reflect the population being studied?

That question arose when Art Klein did his first self-selected study. His landmark survey results about back sufferers formed the basis of *Backache Relief*, published by Times Books in 1985. The survey for that book rated and evaluated a wide range of back practitioners and treatment modalities. There were the expected few objections from medical specialists and drug companies who wanted to be seen in a more positive light. There was the inevitable statement from one medical organization that the research was not based on a random sample or on clinically controlled studies. (Both types of research are far beyond the resources of any individual researcher.) In the end, every major finding of the study was validated. To cite but a few examples, subsequent studies reported in prestigious medial journals showed that:

Exercise was the best form of prevention and treatment for most back sufferers. This finding had been consistently "pooh-poohed" by the medical establishment for decades.

Diagnostic tests such as tomography were dangerous and less precise than modern equipment such as CAT Scans and the then newly developed MRI.

No standard drug treatments were significantly more therapeutic than a placebo.

Chiropractic treatment for chronic lower back pain brought no more than temporary relief for most back sufferers.

The most widely used medical practrioners—orthopedists and neurologists—were among the least effective for most back problems.

Art Klein's next research study, for *Arthritis: What Works*, published by St. Martin's, proved equally prescient and reliable.

We feel confident that the survey for *The Single Parent Resource* is both newsworthy, and more important, truly indicative of the needs, concerns, interests and views of today's single parents.

Sources for self-selection were carefully selected to represent a wide range of the book-buying, help-seeking single-parent population. These sources included publications, Internet related family sites, and news groups for or about dads, women, divorce, child support and single parents.

After our first 100 survey responses, two things became unwaveringly clear:

1. There were some 10 topics that single parents were especially interested in for improving their lives. We based much of the content of our book on these topics.

2. Single parents and their children are being hurt by society's negative view of them. Although this finding has no real practical value to readers, it has significant news value and long-range implications for our nation's ongoing dialogue about families and family values.

Another strong suit: we conducted in-depth interviews from our universe of 500 survey participants. (A remarkable 88% of these participants checked a box to inform us of their willingness to be interviewed!)

A final point. With some self-selected surveys, where participants are paid a cash amount for participating, the true interest of some participants can be questioned. Not so of the people we have surveyed. Their incentive to fill out our survey? Reading materials—three issues of Brook Noel's single-parenting newsletter. In addition, no incentive of any kind was paid for in-depth interviews.

Sex of Respondents:

Male	16%
Female	84%

Reason given by survey respondents for being in a single-parent situation:

Divorced	58%
Widowed	3%
I am a single parent by choice	10%
Unmarried	25%
Other	4%

We asked survey respondents to mark areas that concerned them as a single parent. We also offered areas for single parents to write in their own concerns. The top concerns were:

Managing my single-parent household	80%
Balancing work and family	86%
Maintaining open communication with children	65%
Society's view of single-parent families	47%
Having a good relationship with the other parent	42%
Discussing the single-parent family with my children	46%
Maintaining holidays and special days as happy occasions	50%
Fulfilling my own career goals	65%
Having a solid financial plan and budget system	80%
Finding quality child care	64%
Finding a support network for single parents	69%
Maintaining an active social life	62%
Dating and relationships	67%
Legal issues: custody arrangements, child-support payments and other divorce related matters	47%
Learning how to find more free time	59%
Involving my children in helping around the house and working together as a family	59%
Remarrying	44%
Understanding my child's feelings	77%
Ensuring that my child has the opportunity to have a good relationship with the other parent	42%

Creating smooth transitions and visits	35%
Missing/worrying about my child during visitation periods	36%
Encouraging role models in my child's life	70%
Financial planning for the future	74%
Dealing with my own stress, anger, fatigue and other emotions	83%
Keeping up relationships with friends and family	48%

Of the 500 survey participants,

3% had four or more children
9% had three children
32% had two children
56% had one child

We asked our survey participants a few questions about their social life. Here are the questions and results.

Are you currently dating?
34% Yes
66% No

How many times per month do you go out with a friend without your children?

8 or more times	4%
5-7 times per month	7%
2-4 times per month	28%
Less than twice a month	61%

How many times each month do you go on a date without your children?

8 or more times	2%
5-7 times per month	4%
2-4 times per month	18%
Less than twice a month	76%

We asked our survey participants if they would like our book to tell them any more about any of the following areas that pertain to the social life of a single parent.

Where to meet people	56%
When to introduce children to someone new in your life.	65%
How to deal with children's jealousy, anger and curiosity about your new romantic interest.	64%
How to handle talking to your children about your "significant other" spending the night at your home.	49%
The pros and cons of living together with a romantic interest.	49%
Marrying again.	54%

We asked our survey participants to tell us which of the following phrases best describes their parenting relationship.

The other parent and I share joint custody	9%
I am the custodial parent and my child spends time with the non-custodial parent regularly	25%
I am the custodial parent and my child spends time with the non-custodial parent irregularly	29%
I am the custodial parent and my child does not have a relationship with the other parent	32%
I am the non-custodial parent	2%
I am a widowed parent and primary caregiver	3%

Of our survey participants for whom custodial arrangements were applicable, 53% were satisfied with their current arrangement. 46% were not satisfied. 1% had no opinion. Of those who were satisfied, the majority were those who shared joint custody or had a regular schedule established with the other parent. The majority of those who were least satisfied were custodial parents who reported non-custodial parents that did not see their children regularly. The majority of these custodial parents felt they would be satisfied if a regular schedule was established and upheld.

When asked how our single parent survey respondents thought society views the single-parent family, they reported the following:

The same as the two-parent traditional family.	1%
A new kind of family that is opening people's eyes to different kinds of successful family arrangements.	14%
A family with more problems than most.	40%
A family inferior to the traditional nuclear family.	43%
No opinion	2%

We asked our survey participants to rate on a scale of one to five, (one being strongly agree, five being strongly disagree), how they felt about the following statement. "I feel my community accepts single-parent families."
Using five to strongly disagree and one to strongly agree, here is what they said:

Five (strongly disagree)	10%
Four	18%
Three	32%
Two	23%
One (strongly agree)	14%
No opinion	3%

We asked our survey participants if they felt children in single-parent homes could grow up to be at least as well adjusted as children raised in a traditional two-parent home.
Using five to strongly disagree and one to strongly agree, here is what they said:

Five (strongly disagree)	6%
Four	14%
Three	22%
Two	24%
One (strongly agree)	30%
No opinion	4%

We asked our survey participants to rate how they felt about the following statement on a scale of one to five. "I feel my child is doing better in a single-parent family than he/she would have in our prior family arrangement."
Using five to strongly disagree and one to strongly agree, here is what they said:

Five (strongly disagree)	11%
Four	11%
Three	14%
Two	11%
One (strongly agree)	50%
No opinion	3%

We asked our survey participants how they felt about the following statement, "I feel my child has dealt well with upsetting emotions about living in a single-parent family."
Using five to strongly disagree and one to strongly agree, here is what they said:

Five (strongly disagree)	7%
Four	15%
Three	26%
Two	23%
One (strongly agree)	24%
No opinion	5%

We asked our survey participants how they felt about the following statement, "I feel confident and enjoy my life as a single parent."
Using five to strongly disagree and one to strongly agree, here is what they said:

Five (strongly disagree)	10%
Four	15%
Three	24%
Two	26%
One	22%
No opinion	3%

The single parents in our survey, wanted our book to cover the following issues related to child-rearing:

Understanding children's emotions	78%
Discussing unique differences about single-parent families	75%
Involving children in work around the house	56%
Having more quality time with my children	70%
Teenager sexuality, pregnancy and related issues	44%
Drugs and alcohol	41%
Family Values	68%
The other parent's absence	69%

Of our survey participants 88% volunteered to be interviewed by phone.

The Single Parent Resource
Scholarship Project

A portion of the profits of this book will be awarded as college scholarships to children who are currently living in single-parent homes.

All children who have been accepted to college or will be by March of 1999 are eligible. All entries for the first year of awards must be postmarked by February 1, 1999. Recipients will be notified by May 15, 1999. If you would like to receive notification of the number of scholarships granted, and the recipients, please mail a self addressed stamped envelope to: Award Notification, The Single Parent Resource Scholarship Project, c/o Champion Press, Ltd., 264 S. La Cienega Blvd., Suite 1064, Beverly Hills, CA 90211. Announcements will be mailed by July 1, 1999.

For the entry dates of scholarships after the 1999 awards, please send a self-addressed-stamped-envelope with a request for future scholarship information to Champion Press, Ltd.

All entries will be read by a panel of three judges. The panel includes both authors of *The Single Parent Resource* and a third expert in the field of single-parenting who will be announced each year. Awards will be based on the originality, quality, and thoroughness of a written essay.

Subject: Submit an essay response, typed and double spaced (between 250-1000 words) in response to the following question:

How can we help and encourage the positive growth and recognition of the single-parent family form in society?

The Single Parent Resource cannot be held responsible for lost entries. No relative of the authors, judging panel or Champion Press, Ltd. shall be allowed entry for scholarships.

Each submission must contain two copies of the essay. Each essay must include a cover page containing the essay title, author name and contact information. Only the essay title should appear on subsequent pages. Any manuscript that does not follow this format will be discarded.

No entries can be returned. All entries submitted become the property of *The Single Parent Resource* & Champion Press, Ltd.

Award recipients will be required to verify their single-parent household status upon award of the scholarship. If proof is not provided within 30 days the scholarship will be re-awarded to the next chosen applicant.

Mail submissions to:
The Single-Parent Resource Scholarship Project
c/o Champion Press, Ltd.
264 S. La Cienega Blvd., Suite 1064
Beverly Hills, CA 90211

Bibliography

Brabec, Barbara. *Homemade Money*. Betterway Books, 1994.

Breathnach, Sarah Ban. *Simple Abundance: A Daybook of Comfort and Joy*. New York: Warner, 1995.

Bykofsky, Sheree. *500 Terrific Ideas for Organizing Everything*. New York: Simon & Schuster, 1992.

Card, Emily W., and Christine Watts Kelly. *The Single Parent's Money Guide*. New York: MacMillan, 1996.

Collins, Emily. *The Whole Single Person's Catalog*. Farrar Straus & Giroux, 1979.

Culp, Stephanie. *How To Conquer Clutter*. Cincinnati: Writer's Digest Books, 1989.

Dominguez, Joe, and Vicki Robin. *Your Money or Your Life*. New York: Penguin, 1993.

Engber, Andrea, and Leah Klungness, Ph.D. *The Complete Single Mother*. Holbrook: Adams, 1995.

Foust, Linda. *The Single Parent's Almanac*. Rocklin: Prima, 1996.

Hart, Dr. Archibald D. *Helping Children Survive Divorce*. Dallas: 1997.

Jeffers, Susan, Ph.D. *End The Struggle and Dance With Life*. New York: St. Martin's, 1996.

Krantzler, Mel. *Creative Divorce*. New York: Signet, 1973.

Lansky, Vicki. *Divorce Book for Parents*. Deephaven: Book Peddlers, 1996.

Muro, Rachel. "Theme Dinners." *The Single Parent Resource*, Vol. II, Issue 6.

National Center for Health Statistics. "Advance Report of Final Divorce Statistics, 1989 and 1990." Monthly Vital Statistics Report, Vol. 43, No. 9, Supp. April, 1995.

National Center for Health Statistics. "Births to Unmarried Mothers: United States, 1980-1992." Vital and Health Statistic Series 21, No. 53. June, 1995.

Noel, Carol. *Get It? Got It. Good!*. Petoskey: Serious Business, 1996.

Roesch, Roberta. *The Working Woman's Guide to Managing Time*. Englewood: Prentice Hall, 1996.

Steenhouse, Andrea Van. *A Woman's Guide to a Simpler Life*. New York: Harmony, 1996.

Teyber, Edward. *Helping Children Cope With Divorce*. San Francisco: Jossey-Bass, 1992.

United States. Bureau of the Census. "Child Support for Custodial

Mothers and Fathers: 1991."

United States. Bureau of the Census. "Half of Nation's Children Live In Non-Traditional Families." August, 1994.

United States. Bureau of the Census. "Households and Families." March, 1994.

United States. Bureau of the Census. "Marital Status and Living Arrangements." March, 1994.

United States. Bureau of the Census. "New Census Bureau Report Profiles The State of The Nation." January, 1995.

United States. Bureau of the Census. "Parents Fall Short on Child Support Payments." May, 1995.

United States. Bureau of the Census. "Single Parents Maintain 3 In 10 Family Groups Involving Children." August, 1994.

United States. Department of Commerce. "Who Receives Child Support?" Statistical Brief. May, 1995.

United States. Department of Commerce. "Facts for Father's Day." CB97-FS.06. June, 1997.

United States. Department of Commerce. "Facts for Mother's Day." CB97-FS.05. May, 1997.

United States. Department of Commerce. "Single-Parent Growth Rate Stabilized; 2-Parent Family Growth Renewed, Census Bureau Reports." CB95-186. October, 1995.

United States. Bureau of the Census. "Trends in Marital Composition." November, 1993.

Wagner, Hilory. *The New Parents Sourcebook*. New York, Carol. 1996.

"What I Wish My Parents Knew." *Single Parenting In The Nineties*. Vol. I. 1995.

V
vital records, 257

W
widows, 139
wills, 112-114

Y
YMCA, 53-54

Z
Zero Coupon Bonds, 110

Brook Noel maintains a mailing list for upcoming workshops, book announcements and single-parenting news. To be added to her personal list please fill out (or photocopy) and return this form to Brook Noel, c/o Champion Press, Ltd., 264 S. La Cienega Blvd., Suite 1064, Beverly Hills, CA 90211.

Please note that this information is not sold, rented or distributed in any way. It is for the author's mailing list only and for announcements of Champion Press, Ltd.'s upcoming titles.

Name _____

Address_____Apt._____

City _____

State_____ Zip _____

Country _____

Home Phone Number _____

E-mail address _____

Book purchased _____

Where did you purchase this book_____

The author is available for workshops and speaking engagements. For more information, please write to Champion Press, Ltd. at the address above.

Visit the web site of
Champion Press, Ltd.
for upcoming book information,
tour information,
and the
Single Parent Resource Reading Room!

http://www.championpress.com

EDUCATIONAL AND GROUP DISCOUNTS ARE AVAILABLE FOR
MORE INFORMATION WRITE TO CHAMPION PRESS, LTD.

Please photocopy this page to order additional copies of *The Single Parent Resource*. Or to order on the other titles by the authors. Or order on-line at our web site, www.championpress.com.

QUANTITY

_____   *The Single Parent Resource*, by Brook Noel
with Art Klein. $13.95

_____   *Shadows Of A Vagabond*, by Brook Noel. $12

_____   *Dad and Son* by Art Klein. $12.95

_____   Shipping and handling. $2.95 for the first book and $1 more for
each additional book

_____   Payment enclosed

_____   Please charge my ___ Visa ___ MasterCard

Account Number _____

Expiration Date _____

Signature _____

Name as it appears on card _____

Name _____

Address _____

City _____ State _____ Zip _____

Day Phone _____

Autograph Copy   Yes ____ No ____ Personalize to: _____

MAIL FORM TO:

Champion Press, Ltd.

264 S. La Cienega Blvd., Suite 1064

Beverly Hills, CA 90211